The History of Educational Ideas

in the West

The History of Educational Ideas
in the West

WILLIAM K. MEDLIN

Associate Professor
School of Education
The University of Michigan

The Center for Applied Research in Education, Inc.
New York

Foreword

A physician can be a good physician and a scientist an effective scientist without knowing much about the history of their professions. The frontiers of their knowledge are so rapidly expanding that there is little time for looking back.

Yet, it seems characteristic of outstanding men in the applied as well as in the theoretical sciences that they gratefully acknowledge the merits of their predecessors and seek to understand the evolution of their disciplines. The historical perspective deepens their sense of belonging, widens their horizons, and produces new associations that stimulate further inquiry.

This is all the more true in the case of the humanities, of which, from my point of view, education is an integral part. (What study and activity could be more concerned with *homo* and *humanitas* than education?) Although for the rapidly accumulating sciences the present may to some extent have surpassed the past, in the humanities the past is ever vividly present. With the exception of those intellectual and spiritual achievements that may have been totally lost (I doubt that there are many), the thoughts of bygone generations are interwoven in our own modes of thinking and living. There are still with us the ideas and aspirations of the Jews, the Greeks and the Romans, the early Christians and medieval scholars, the Renaissance and the Reformation, the Enlightenment and the philosophers and naturalists of the eighteenth and nineteenth centuries.

Each of these movements has affected the aims and contents of education. Indeed, the more the teaching in our schools extends from regional, even from typically Western concepts to global aspects—vertical and horizontal—the more are we torn between our feeling of deficiency in knowledge and the intellectual demands of the present and the future. Anthropology, genetic psychology, and—last, but not least—the frightening political and racial hatreds and persecutions in our immediate environment have taught us that

the old myths and seemingly buried superstitions of aborigines still
live in the parents of some schoolchildren. And whereas a few
decades ago Africa was for most of us a distant continent, and the
cultures of Asia a matter for experts, today the American teacher
has to prepare citizens of a country that cannot properly discharge
its international obligations unless it understands the mentality of
the inhabitants of ever widening geographical and experiential
orbits. And this understanding—as we have learned from bitter
political disappointments—requires not only a knowledge of what
foreign people are, but also a knowledge of how they have become
what they are; in other words, a knowledge of their intellectual and
spiritual heritage.

Particularly, we cannot simply transfer our American forms of
education to foreign countries, even if in their impatience they demand quick procedures. If we do, we damage them and ourselves.

It would, of course, be ridiculous if we asked young students or
even mature teachers of the history of education to be at home in the
enormous expanse of the history of humanity. Today no one completely masters even his own specialty. But what we must ask is that
the American teacher acquire a sense of the magnitude of human
problems and of their effects on education.

This sense, I believe, can best be developed during a prospective
teacher's student years, when he is not hurried by the tasks which
will confront him during his professional career. And this development can best be fostered by exposing him, with occasional
comparative excursions, to the history of his own cultural and educational situation—*non multa sed multum*. The roots must grow
with the tree.

We should, therefore, welcome the decision of a man of Professor Medlin's professional experience to write the present volume on
the history of educational ideas in the West within the broader
framework of the Library of Education. He modestly calls his book
a "survey." Indeed, if measured against all that could be told about
the subject, no endeavor could achieve completeness. However,
Professor Medlin's volume will give the student so much to con-
template that he will think of it as a source of enrichment and use
it as a starting point from which to wander farther into the wide
landscape of professional education.

ROBERT ULICH

The History of Educational Ideas
in the West

William K. Medlin

No doctor would think of prescribing therapy for the ills of a patient before getting the patient's clinical record. Neither should educators think of prescribing for the shortcomings of education without getting the clinical record or case history of education. Although a patient's case history may go back a generation or two at the most, that of education goes back centuries, even millennia. Professor Medlin shows in this volume not only how old the present is but also how contemporaneous is the past.

If anyone has any doubt on the contemporaneity of the past let him read two voices from the past:

> Our earth is degenerate in these latter days. There are signs that the world is coming to an end. Children no longer obey their parents.

> The children now love luxury, they have bad manners, contempt for authority, they show disrespect for elders, and love chatter in place of exercise. Children are now tyrants, not the servants of their households. They no longer rise when elders enter the room. They contradict their parents, chatter before company, gobble up dainties at the table, cross their legs, and tyrannize over their teachers.

The first statement was made 6000 years ago by an Egyptian priest and the second was made by Socrates 2500 years ago! These statements should afford no cause for taking comfort but they should help the current generation to keep its poise and perspective in a period when critics of contemporary education seem to think they are making similar indictments for the first time.

So voluminous has the history of both the past and even the recent past become that the author has felt the need of terminating his account at the end of the nineteenth century at which point another volume of the Library of Education will take up the story.

JOHN S. BRUBACHER
Content Editor

vii

Contents

CHAPTER I

Education in Classical Mediterranean Civilizations

Introduction: Educational History as a Field of Inquiry

The reflections men make on educational traditions, as well as the records of those traditions themselves, constitute educational history. Educational history has been a part of European historical literature since Greek and Roman times, when a Hesiod, a Plato, or a Cicero put down his ideas about the ways in which his forefathers had brought up their children. As a mode of thought and criticism, educational history has followed the same canons of scholarship as similar endeavors in the areas of history, humanistic studies, and social sciences. Times and traditions have variously conditioned the emphasis, the subject, or the rules. But as Collingwood has so well put it in *The Idea of History*, it is what the historian perceives as important that makes history worthwhile. Perhaps this is one of the charms of change.

So the Greek poet wrote with a view to creating a new social philosophy, and he interpreted the past in a way favorable to changing educational practices. Plato drew from historical experience an ideal model in the hope of saving his civilization. An eighteenth-century man of progress, such as Condorcet, saw in history a gradual fulfillment of mankind's destiny to perfect the human condition—an evolutionary process in which education had a vital role.

The history of education, like all history, can thus be dressed in different garb, according to the writer's purpose. There arises then a question: *Why* do men view history in different ways? That they are profoundly moved by ideas and toward ideas is evident in their writings; but *how* do they come to espouse particular ideas and purposes, rather than others?

It is one of the several tasks of historians to inquire into the ideas and actions of men and their institutions, in order that they may explain them as well as describe them. Historical studies have abundantly shown that the milieu in which men move—the natural, social, and intellectual climate or environment—is the crucible for thought and action. The investigations of the behavioral sciences into human society over the past one hundred years provide mountains of confirming data. Social man is indelibly linked with his times, and he is in a sense a cultural product of traditions undergoing change. Rousseau recognized this situation when he remarked that though man is born naturally free, he is immediately in chains —linked to his surroundings. Man's responses to his environment and to changes in it create new cultures—new social relationships and new value commitments. The quality of his responses, in terms of his needs and goals, determines the quality of his culture.

The various solutions to the problem of educating youth during the history of the Western tradition are, essentially, descriptions of European man's cultural responses to his changing environment. Some of the solutions, such as the Platonic, were never really experimented with in terms of their total meaning and context. So far as educational history is concerned, then, the real response in education to the crisis-ridden Greek culture of the fourth century, both theoretically and practically, was the educational programs that survived the times. That is not to say that Plato had no influence in his own day or in later history. It is in the question about influence that the historian comes to grips with the philosopher's response, so that his original thesis takes on meaning.

Education, then, must be studied as a function of culture, defined as the set of values and habits governing human behavior. If this cultural definition departs from more traditional intellectual views, it is the author's belief that it does so in name only. What may well appear to be a material interest or a habit perpetuated by educational process can, and should, really be seen as a thought-form. By this method, one acknowledges that every human incidence and circumstance has, as its real, an intellectual expression or set of expressions. This view gives to educational history a uniquely dynamic character, explaining how man institutes changes in his culture and social relationships. Education—the school—is an agent of thought-forms, and the history of education is the record of sociocultural change, whether in children who must conform to adult values or among adults who must accept new forms of culture. Where in fact there is no change or movement, there is nothing to report—no "history." And such wastelands in our human past do indeed exist.

This interpretation of educational history is not intended to be anti-idealistic, nor is it meant to be materially or culturally deterministic. Depending on the level of cultural development, idealistic values may range high or low in their importance for human activities. Those who manage the culture—those social leaders who ultimately determine the reward-and-punishment system—generally decide the kind of educational solution society will have. That Plato's scheme has never been implemented as originally conceived does not mean it never can or never will.

Because of the multitude of "solutions" to man's educational needs that have evolved through the centuries, it is impossible for this volume to present any analysis that might be termed comprehensive. The treatment will be highly selective: first, in terms of the magnitude of the change in educational thought at particular times in history; second, in terms of geographic areas (with Europe as the major concern); and third, with respect to chronological emphasis, which falls on the historical periods of greatest cultural achievement. These criteria are arbitrary, but the resulting selections appear to offer the most interest in view of the educational problems in the Western world today.

The European tradition moved, both in ancient times and during the Christian era, from tribal culture to complex, urban, sophisticated culture with highly developed educational institutions. Europe has been the most productive area in the world of educational ideas, and therefore it furnishes a natural focal point excluding other major cultural systems. European confrontation with these other systems in the contemporary world, however, is a matter of real educational concern.

For reasons of both space and methodology, the discussion here terminates essentially with the mid-nineteenth century. Educational thought reflecting different philosophical doctrines and expressing various cultural and national traditions are discussed in other volumes of this Library.

The main purpose of such a review of educational history is not only to provide information on who did or wrote what or when, but to provide an intellectual experience through which the reader can relate the task of education to society's interests at different times and under various circumstances. It should enable him to develop the habit of perceiving such relationships by organizing information in such a way that the relation between educational change and sociocultural change becomes demonstrable. The literature on educational history has long been working toward this goal, and it is hoped that this small contribution continues the trend in this direction.[1]

Western civilization is in its second historical period of creative expansion. The first great burgeoning of literary, philosophical, and scientific culture in ancient Greece and Rome produced a set of educational institutions that remained unequalled until recent times. The real nature of this early achievement, and its comparison with modern education, deserve attention that lies beyond this paper's scope. But, for this reason, some emphasis has been put on early European ideas—perhaps to the detriment of more popular ideas and times. History may one day judge this choice.

Ancient Resources of
the Western Tradition

Education in the first "modern" civilizations of the Near East

> I have taught you statutes and judgments . . . ; teach them thy sons, and thy sons' sons.
>
> *Moses*

The millennium after 5000 B.C. marked the gradual rise of sedentary and then urban cultures in the valleys of the Tigris-Euphrates (Mesopotamia) and the Nile.[1a] Possibilities for agriculture as well

---

1 On the subject see, for example, W. Burnham and H. Suzzalo, *The History of Education as a Professional Subject* (New York: Teachers College, Bureau of Publications, Columbia University, 1908); "New Emphasis on History of Education in Response to War and Postwar Demands," in *XXIX Yearbook,* National Society of College Teachers of Education; and Committee on Historical Foundations, *The Role of the History of Education in the Professional Preparation of Teachers* (Ann Arbor: National Society of College Teachers of Education, 1957).

1a The sites of other ancient cultures, such as the Indus, Yangtze, and Oxus (modern Turkistan) regions, whose early civilizations are interesting indeed, cannot be considered here.

The author extends his genuine thanks to Professors John S. Brubacher and Robert Ulich for their cooperation.

as nomadism and other forms of food-gathering created wealth and new social functions in human relations. These new functions called for a more formal initiation of the young into adult life. Imitation of parents and apprenticeship were insufficient to meet the needs and interests of urban dwellers. Evidences of these social changes are particularly rich in the ruins of ancient cities of Sumeria, where archeological finds since the late nineteenth century have written a new chapter in cultural history.

As one of the great centers of urban production and commerce, Sumeria and its successors created a civilization that required many kinds of formal education and training. Many of the values of Sumerian culture are familiar to us today in our own society; among these are respect for individual property (although in theory all land was owned by the gods), regulations governing trade, a system of municipal laws, and respect for public and religious authorities. Certain other traditions, however, such as the deification of human beings and the religious, sacerdotal nature of certain ruling authorities are at variance with modern American values. The thousands of clay tablets dug up over the past seventy-five years have given us a most detailed account of this early Sumerian culture.[2] This information includes considerable data on the educational affairs and interests of that time. Its importance lies principally in the fact that these people, and their cultural heirs, had broad influence on the neighboring European and Semitic tribes that lived and moved about the crossroads of the three great continents.

Sumerian society developed a number of special functions and services which required trained individuals for their performance. Besides governors, city councillors (elders), and ambassadorial personnel, there were accountants, work supervisors (or foremen), military officers, temple administrators, archivists, and recorders.[3] Usually called *scribes,* all these officials required some general education—especially reading, writing, and counting—and special training. It seems historically logical that writing skills constituted

[2] Samuel N. Kramer, *History Begins at Sumer* (Garden City, N.Y.: Doubleday & Company, Inc., 1959), pp. xixff.; Thomas Woody, *Life and Education in Early Societies* (New York: The Macmillan Company, 1949), pp. 77ff.

[3] *Ibid.,* pp. 1–2; Henri I. Marrou, *Histoire de l'education dans l'antiquité* (Paris: Editions du Seuil, 1948), pp. 19–21. Cultural achievements in the intellectual, scientific, artistic, and political fields, which seem to be coincident with educational development at Sumer, merit investigation.

the earliest formal educational curriculum, and that they developed from the need to account for numbers of people, goods, or commercial transactions. The Sumerian scribes had to learn to classify words according to their function, such as rural, urban, animal, mineral—classifications that suggest a kind of "subject matter" approach to learning.

Teaching was organized under a senior or master teacher, who supervised a number of assistants and special instructors. Perhaps the best idea of how Sumerian schools operated and of their relative importance at that time can be gleaned from some of the tablets unearthed at Sumer. They described the schools and formal learning processes conducted between 3000 and 2000 B.C.

PROGRAM OF STUDY FOR A SCHOOL DAY[4]

Question: What did you do in school?
Pupil: I recited my tablet, ate my lunch, prepared my [new] tablet, wrote it, finished it; then they assigned me my oral work, and in the afternoon they assigned me my written work.

PUPIL–TEACHER RELATIONSHIPS[5]

Pupil: ... I went to school. In school the monitor in charge said to me. . . .
Monitor: Why are you late?
Pupil: Afraid and with pounding heart, I entered before my teacher and made a respectful curtsy. [School work begins.]
Teacher: Your hand [copy] is not satisfactory. [Thereupon the teacher caned the pupil.]

From this brief dialogue, it is clear that in ancient Sumeria pupils were at times supervised by monitors—perhaps senior pupils or young apprentice teachers. Apparently, their tasks included taking the roll and attending to the proper seating or grouping of the youngsters. The use of physical as well as verbal threats indicates that fear was the school-inspired motivation for learning and behaving. The teacher, as master of the schoolroom, had full authority over the child and directly imposed adult control. The nature of this role shows that one principal purpose of education was to pass on the adult cultural heritage, and that the teacher enjoyed consider-

---

4 Kramer, *op. cit.,* pp. 8–9.
5 *Ibid.,* p. 9.

able community confidence in this task. The head teacher had an assistant who was himself preparing for the teaching role, a fact which reflects the rather high level of social development achieved by the teaching function in that society.

The tablets found in Mesopotamia provide other data which make it possible to reconstruct more of the Sumerian educational system and the theory behind it. The "copybooks" of students indicate that there was a series of graded steps, from elementary to advanced, in reading and writing exercises, through which pupils passed. As the student progressed, the subject matter he studied increased in difficulty and variety. The subjects included grammar; rural, urban, natural, and physical affairs; and arithmetic. The evidence available suggests that the more advanced literary studies were almost exclusively concerned with poetic works: myths, epic tales about heroes and gods, hymns, lamentations, proverbs, fables, and essays.[6] Advanced students learned to write and recite these works as well as their teachers did, and so qualified to become either scribes in the clerical hierarchy serving the state or managerial officials in the military, financial, records, or commercial service. Perhaps some of the graduates of these schools became themselves teachers or headmasters.

These few but essential data fill in a significant chapter in educational history, at the dawn of what is now called the Western tradition. They describe an institution of education that is quite familiar in many ways: an educational structure of at least two levels, elementary and advanced, divided into a series of academic steps; a psychological use of threat, punishment, and reward (or promise of professional status) to induce learning and desired behavior; pre-professional preparation of youth for adult roles in religious, business, and state functions; a foyer both for learning and for developing literary traditions, that the culture might be carried on and enriched; parental support of and interest in the school; high community regard for the teaching role; and last, but not least, a system for training future teachers—a service essential to the improvement of the educational institution as well to its perpetuation.

Undoubtedly inspired by the growth and needs of an urban culture, Sumerian education is an outstanding example of man's early efforts to develop an institution to perfect the human condition. In

---

[6] *Ibid.*, p. 5.

this sense it forms part of a long humanistic tradition. Although the Sumerian schools failed to withstand the ravages of time and the pressures of migrating peoples, they influenced newcomers and neighbors, who carried their learning further west, to the Mediterranean basin.

The educational achievements of the Egyptians are reported in detail in other surveys.[7] However, a word on the educational ideas of the Hebrews, whose impact on religious and social teachings in the West need not be elaborated upon, will be useful here.

Hebrew education was based on the patriarchal writings (the Old Testament), which contained the laws for governing the people of Israel. The patriarchs commanded, in behalf of the one God, that these laws be taught from generation to generation (e.g., Deut. 4:1, 28:4). Their study and application were deemed to build moral character through obedience to principles of honesty, purity, humility, family honor, and community solidarity. The system was based on the idea that the believers were a chosen people whose duty was to glorify God and whose destiny was to inherit the earth; and this concept has continued to be a powerful influence in the Judeo-Christian world. It has been a philosophy of history explaining the main purposes of life and the rewards attainable by those without sin. This ethic distinguished Hebrew teachings from other ancient and classical educational thought. It did not so much inspire a search for knowledge or truth as it encouraged the effort toward faith and righteousness. This feature was well expressed in the prophecy of Daniel concerning the four great kingdoms, the last of which would be God-chosen: "... a kingdom which shall never be destroyed: and the kingdom shall not be left to other people, but it shall ... consume all these kingdoms, and it shall stand forever" (Daniel 2:44).

Jewish educational ideas can perhaps be briefly explained in two terms: character education and a social ethic. Both ideas embody a divine and historical purpose. All educational efforts, directed by the priests and kings, aimed at these goals rather than at the development of human science and new knowledge. Here was an early and fundamental difference between Judaic educational thought and other systems (especially the Greek), which tended to be more

---

[7] E.g., see James Mulhern, *A History of Education,* 2nd. ed. (New York: The Ronald Press Company, 1959), Chap. 3; and Woody, *op. cit.,* Chap. 3.

pragmatic and conducive to change. In the subsequent history of Western education, both tendencies can be seen in the cultures of new social systems arising out of, or in some way related to, the societies of the ancient world.

Greek Ideas of Education and
Culture (Paideia)
ca. 1600–300 B.C.

> . . . I was set by him to instruct thee as my son, that thou might-est speak, when speech was fit, and do, when deeds were done. . . .
>
> *Phoenix to Achilles*

Early background and environment. The cultural achievement that was classical Greece, whose educational models have been a hallmark of the Western tradition, was generated by those adventuresome and inquisitive Indo-Europeans inhabiting the peninsular, insular, and coastal Asian regions bathed by the Aegean Sea.[8] The Greeks' geographic position had no little influence on their rise to leadership and on their development of educational ideas. It protected them from invasion by land, gave them access to maritime commerce and foreign expansion, and permitted them to develop cultural contacts with the rest of the known world.

This relative security and easy communication were indeed partly responsible for the rise of civilizations in the peninsula and island communities during the second millennium B.C. Under these conditions, the Greeks could grow, expand, study, and create. By 500–300 B.C., the Greeks emerged as the chief founders of the European intellectual, humanistic, and scientific tradition. With the later infusion of Judeo-Christian religious ideas, the Europeans received the main civilizational tools and materials with which they could educate themselves further and create an even higher culture.

The Greeks were a part of those Indo-European pastoral tribes which, as they slowly moved westward, developed an epic poetry recording the tribal exploits of yore. Courage and success enshrined warrior and chieftain for posterity and reinforced an aristocratic

---

[8] References here to historical Greek traditions in education will be more general than specific, but the writer does not mean thereby to obscure the diversity that was characteristic among the many Greek city-states. By the nature of this volume, however, and because the Greeks did not exhibit considerable cultural unity, the emphasis will be on the common features.

tradition that, along with the office of elder, was the essence of social leadership within these tribes. Aristocratic leadership and its required qualities were also taught by the legends and myths.[9] The religious rites honoring household and nature gods were centered in the home, with the father as main performer whom all had to respect. The tribal peasantry, pastoral and agricultural, depended upon the warrior-nobles for protection.

In Greece, the growth of sedentary agriculture and of aristocratic rule based on obedience to family traditions led, in the second millennium B.C., to the establishment of a kingship system and gradually to the development of an urban civilization and a high culture typified by the glory of Mycenae (which was no doubt in touch with civilizations in Crete and the Near East).[10] It was to the edification of human culture in this early Greek period that the *Iliad* and *Odyssey* of Homer (c. 809–724 B.C.)—two of the most influential educational documents ever written in a European language—were dedicated. Although the period from about 1200 B.C. to Homer's time, dominated by the invading Dorian Greeks (who apparently crushed Mycenaean civilization), is referred to as the "dark age" of early Greece, it witnessed a cultural and social growth similar to that of the Mycenaean period. Homeric epics describing the heroic life of aristocratic chivalry of the early civilization were seemingly appropriate to the interests of Greek society of his time and, by cultural transmission, to certain interests of succeeding generations. A renewal of Greek writing by the borrowing of letters from the Phoenicians (according to present evidence) enhanced the educational role that Homer (and, after him, Hesiod) played. In a sense, Mycenaean history merged with that of Homeric and "modern" Greece—at least, it was so taught.

Early ideas in Greek education and culture. That kings and nobles were descended from the gods was a precept in early Greek life and culture. This alleged ancestry gave those social leaders an

---

9 William R. Halliday, *Indo-European Folk Tales and Greek Legend* (Cambridge, England: Cambridge University Press, 1933), esp. Chaps. I and IV; also, George D. Thomson, *Studies in Ancient Greek Society*, Vol. I: *The Prehistoric Aegean* (London: Lawrence & Wishart, 1949).

10 J. O. Bury, *A History of Greece to the Death of Alexander*, 3rd ed., rev. by R. Meiggs (London: Macmillan and Company, 1955), pp. 41ff.; Emmett Bennett, *The Pylos Tablets*, rev. ed. (Princeton, N.J.: Princeton University Press, 1955); Michael Ventris and John Chadwick, *Documents in Mycenaean Greek* (Cambridge, England: Cambridge University Press, 1956).

eminence the qualities of which were the subjects of education for all Greek noble boys. Inscribed in the poetry of Homer, this education held a high place in ancient Greece by virtue of Homeric literature's role in schooling (attested to by Plato himself almost four hundred years after Homer).[11] And even more than a thousand years later, the reading of Homer was a part of Byzantine Greek education.

Homer relates to his readers that a man's highest achievement is the development of an excellent character and great courage. Loyalty to and steadfastness in honoring one's family and traditions, obedience to the will of the gods, loyalty to the king, and the courage to prove oneself a skilled and undaunted warrior in the defense of home and country—these were the goals in education for the wellborn boy. They included the understanding of right and wrong necessary for success in aristocratic life and leadership, as well as the fundamental technical and social skills required in daily life. The gods, it was believed, watched over their human family to see that the proper experiences and education were provided.

> In Homer, the real mark of the nobleman is his sense of duty. He is judged, and is proud to be judged, by a severe standard. And the nobleman educated others by presenting to them an eternal ideal, to which they have a duty to conform. . . . The nobleman's pride in high race and ancient achievement is partnered by his knowledge that his pre-eminence can be guaranteed only by the virtues which won it. . . . The hero's whole life and effort are a race for the first prize, an unceasing strife for supremacy over his peers.[12]

This was the essence of ancient Greek education; it set the tone for the great Greek tradition and formed the base of European culture. The goals of goodness, perfection, and form became in time the Greek ideal in education: *kalokagathia* (the quality of being a fine, graceful, and good man),[13] embodying both ethical and esthetic values.

Content and methodology. Education was based on following the example of adults and the gods, and on learning the poems and myths passed down from generation to generation. Historical knowl-

---

[11] Plato, *The Republic,* in *The Works of Plato,* B. Jowett, trans. (New York: The Dial Press, Inc., n.d.), p. 378.

[12] Werner Jaeger, *Paideia: The Ideals of Greek Culture,* Vol. I: *Archaic Greece: The Mind of Athens,* G. Highet, trans. (New York: Oxford University Press, 1960), p. 7.

[13] Marrou, *op. cit.,* p. 78.

edge, whether inscribed in poetry or preserved by oral traditions in family and clan, was part of this early "curriculum." The content of the great epic poems reveals that the protagonists were conscious of historical events and traditions. The instruction Homer transmitted through their speeches had a normative function for youth's behavior.

The gods hover above both Achilles and Telemachus, young nobles whose education includes divine guidance and human trials (punishments for misconduct) that lead to eminence.[14] Young Telemachus receives an education in manly courage and wisdom worthy of a king from the goddess Athena, whose spirit guides him in all his preparations for adult responsibilities.[15] This guidance, together with his experiences, form his "school," and the pattern he follows is recorded in detail by Homer for his own generation and for those to come:

[*Athena:*] Now listen closely to me.
Tomorrow call a meeting of all the Achaean lords
And have your say with the gods as your witnesses. . . .
Man your best ship with twenty oarsmen
And go see what you can learn of your missing father, . . .
Or you may hear the very voice of God, which most often
Informs the hearts of men.
[*Telemachus:*] Friend, You surely speak as a man of great good will,
As a father would speak to his son, and I'll never forget
What you have said.
[*A Greek nobleman:*] Telemachus, truly the gods are teaching your tongue
To vaunt and be bold. May the son of Cronos never
Make you king here in sea-circled Ithaca, though king
You were born to be:[16]

Supernatural wisdom instructs the young elect, whose illustrious heritage fits him for an education from one of the highest of tutors—Athena, the mentor of aristocratic men. He also receives training at the courts and hearths in other lands, developing the practical skills as well as the mental fortitude needed for his calling.

The many examples of military prowess, combining mental keenness with physical and technical skills, which abound in the *Iliad*,

---

14 Jaeger, *op. cit.*, pp. 31, 41.
15 *The Odyssey of Homer*, Ennis Rees, trans. (New York: Random House, 1960), pp. 8, 10–12, 14, 26ff.
16 *Ibid.*, pp. 14–15.

were readymade lessons for Homeric youth. Nestor and Cheiron were great tutors who trained their noble charges in the best techniques of their tradition. Homer relates how Agamemnon sought aid for the wounded Menelaus and describes in detail the military traits and medical skills required of the true warrior.[17] Beautifully embroidered with metaphors from nature, the battle between Aias and Simoeisis tells not only of the tragic fall of a hero but also of the style of life among the Greeks. These realistic literary forms must have had, for a young Greek, particular educational values. These accounts, and many others in the Homeric epics, served not only as examples of behavior for young Greeks to *imitate,* but also as artistic and intellectual creations which, when heard from the lips of a seasoned storyteller or bard, touched the heart and mind of the aspiring nobleman. They formed an *aristocratic* model, justified both by high ancestry and by divine mythology, according to which each generation of leaders educated the next. In addition to studying the arts of command and courage, the young men also learned oratorical skills. Homer describes "the elders of the people . . . excellent speakers still, and clear, as cicadas who through the forest settled on trees, to issue their delicate voice of singing."[18] By a stretch of the imagination, one could say that Homeric literature, as instructional material, served much the same purpose as does modern instruction in civics, morality, English, history, and religion. Only the standards of education at that time were set so high as to be in fact incomparable with those of mass education today. In a larger sense, the poems had an over-all design and purpose: to teach great ethical lessons.

The romantic theme, perhaps as important as the others, was based on the role and charm of woman, and Homer rendered these qualities in a manner that has served as precept to European literary traditions. In the *Iliad,* the abduction of Helen by Paris is made the cause of the Trojan War. Whether historical fact or not, this device emphasizes the place of woman in the culture; and in many ways, both in the *Iliad* and in the *Odyssey,* women are given eminent roles in social affairs and are made not only mistresses of courts or households but also admirable symbols of culture. Beauty and

---

[17] *The Iliad of Homer,* Richmond Lattimore, trans. (Chicago: The University of Chicago Press, 1961), pp. 118–19 (Book IV, 212–19). Copyright 1951 by The University of Chicago Press.

[18] *Ibid.,* p. 104 (III, 150–52).

grace lay at the foundation of this symbolism, and a male-dominated society felt its feminine portent. The following passage, idealizing the fair Helen, provides an example:

Now to Helen of the white arms came a messenger, Iris, . . .
Iris of the swift feet stood beside her and spoke to her:
'Come with me, dear girl, to behold the marvelous things done
by Trojans, breakers of horses, and bronze-armoured Achaians,
who just now carried sorrowful war against each other,
in the plain, and all their desire was for deadly fighting;
now they are all seated in silence, the fighting has ended;
they lean on their shields, the tall spears stuck in the
    ground beside them.
But Menelaos the warlike and Alexandros will fight
with long spears against each other for your possession.
You shall be called beloved wife of the man who wins you.'[19]

A different aspect of culture and education in early Greece is shown in the works of Hesiod (*c.* 753–608 B.C.). Of humble shepherd background, Hesiod portrayed both the traditional values of a "higher" education and the cultural values and social complaints of the hard-working peasantry. He expressed an agrarian morality buttressed by the virtues of toil, thrift, and honesty. This cultural message offers a real contrast with that pervading the gentry-idealizing works of Homer. Although, like Homer, Hesiod is generally concerned with justice, he appeals for a new social justice to correct the inequities of aristocratic rule and to provide a means for the humble to rise to high culture (normally kept as the preserve of the wellborn). In a society that had developed a rigid class structure—an hereditary nobility, a laboring peasantry (free, but often hired on gentry estates), and a slave class—it was natural that social antagonisms would find literary expression, especially since both divine and aristocratic ideals were founded on the principle of justice. Hesiod tells us that the common folk listened to the rhapsodists who sang of the great moral lessons taught by the gods through their chosen human actors. It was right that the gods tell the truth, reasoned Hesiod, so why no mortals?

Here is seen a new cultural theme in Greece—one which reflects intellectual mobility and a changing social scene. Hesiod's main work, *Works and Days,* is a vivid account of the life and values of

---

19 *Ibid.,* pp. 103–104 (III, 121–75, *passim*). Reprinted by permission of The University of Chicago Press.

the agrarian-centered society of Boeotia, a fairly typical Greek community.[20] First causes are still attributed to the gods, but the reader senses a dialectic process: there is tension and movement and a spirit of cultural reconstruction.

This feeling is also manifest in Hesiod's other important work, *Descent of the Gods,* which attempts "to arrange all mythology into a comprehensive philosophical system."[21] His practical, peasant mind was working for a new unity, sensing that somehow there was a more perfect system:

> Driven by the awakening urge to find a due cause for each event, he constructed an ingenious genealogical tree for all the inhabitants of heaven and hell. In his mythical description of Chaos (yawning empty space), of Earth and Heaven (the foundation and roof of the world, separated by Chaos), and of Eros (the cosmic force which creates life), we cannot fail to see the three essential elements of a rational cosmogony. Earth and Heaven are inevitable elements in any such account of the world; and Chaos, which also appears in Nordic myths, is clearly an idea native to the Indo-Germanic[22] race. But Hesiod's Eros is a philosophical conception of his own: a new idea which was to have profoundly stimulating effects on later speculation.[23]

Hesiod thus experienced, and prepared his readers to experience, a new psychological and philosophical—including a dialectical—dimension. His writings and teachings mark the dawn of "modern" thought in Greece, which by the seventh century B.C. was entering a creative and changing cultural period.

Any summary of the long "heroic" period of Greece (from the glorious Mycenaean times to about the eighth century B.C.—perhaps a thousand years) should stress those educational ideas and cultural concepts which seem to be most indicative of Greek cultural values and styles and which have long served to influence European theories of education. The cardinal principles that emerged were:

1. Man must acquire wisdom and knowledge in order to express himself and reach decisions.

---

[20] See Jaeger, *op. cit.,* Vol. I, Chap. 4.

[21] *Ibid.,* p. 65.

[22] In the author's opinion, *Indo-European* is a more appropriate term; and the word *race* is mistaken here; we refer to the *Caucasoid race,* but to the *European peoples.*

[23] Jaeger, *op. cit.,* Vol. I, p. 65. Reprinted by permission of Oxford University Press.

2. Man must acquire the skill to transfer ideas and judgments into action.

3. Man must seek morality, goodness, and virtue.

These concepts of education are embodied in the training of both Achilles and Telemachus. They are simple, but great—and they reflect the Greek's main cultural concern: the defense of family, property, and homeland or tribe. These purposes required strength, bravery, technical skill, persistence, reverence, duty, honor, and sheer will. But all these purposes and qualities were based on supreme life-goals: the perfection of noble qualities and traits in the individual, and the edification of justice, over which the gods arbitrated. The later cultural impact of the peasantry brought this supreme value closer to the social surface. It became a goal of education to harmonize passions, feelings, and personal concern with a high sense of virtue, the ability to distinguish right from wrong, and the will to do what must be done. The final test came on the field of battle and in public office—in other words, in social service. It was thus necessary for education to deal with the mental, the moral, and the physical aspects of the individual. These main ingredients of the Greek theory of education were worked out in the heroic period; modern Greece would refine their forms and broaden their social contexts.

Educational ideas in early and modern (classical) Greece. The maturing and flowering of a culture, and the development of an advanced educational system, do not occur overnight. So it was with Greece, whose own "dark ages" and renaissance seem—in historical perspective—to have prepared the way for an "explosion" of cultural life now identified as the European heritage. The questioning and the search for order and system that marked Hesiod's works were harbingers of future change.

The early heralds of culture and education for all Greece were the poet-bards and poet-writers who, from the end of the eighth century B.C., literally flooded Greek ears with their verses and songs. They were the "teachers" of budding Greek culture. The birth of such writers as Callinus (c. 728), Terpander (c. 712), Alcman (c. 708), Archilochus (c. 705), who were followed by others (Tyrtaeus, Arion, Stesichorus, Alcaeus, Aesop), in the seventh century, marked the emergence of the new era. Their work, together with that of Homer and Hesiod, marked the long period of intellectual and artistic creativity that preceded the actual development of critical, rational, and speculative thought with its accompanying educational fulfillment.

Based largely on this literature, education for the young nobility in Greece was essentially concerned with chivalrous or military values and was largely effected through tutorial methods, often involving intimate relationships between teacher and pupil.[24] At the end of the ninth century B.C., however, Sparta established schools for military and civic education. Physical training occupied first place in this scheme, aiming to give, on the *palestra* (sports field), a well-rounded athletic personality and physique through practice in running, jumping, discus- and javelin-throwing, boxing, and wrestling. Esthetic education was provided through music (also closely related to physical development), which included instruction in dancing, singing, and instrumental music (lyre). These two basic elements of the curriculum, athletics and music, reveal the Greeks' attachment to bodily grace and their appreciation for the fine and the harmonious.

Another subject was literature (poetry and lyrics, mainly), which was taught somewhat informally by those skilled in storytelling and singing, and by participants in the symposia—gatherings for relaxation and entertainment. Training for adulthood took place, of course, in the family and in military and governing circles. Particularly at Sparta did they emphasize the training necessary for soldiering and for command.

For several hundred years Spartan military and civic culture was prominent in Greek educational thought, leaving a heritage for later thinkers, including Plato, to evaluate. Largely because of their policy of dominating and enslaving the indigenous population, Spartan aristocratic rulers devised a rigorous education to train hardy—but unthinking—soldiers. Strenuous physical exercises toughened the body and trained the reflexes. Musical art was not neglected;[25] the military and civic functions that allowed Spartans to display their physical skills were also forums for budding artists:

> When sacrifices were made to the city's tutelary deities there were solemn processions . . . like those of the Hyacinthia, in which

---

[24] The tutorship practice, with its particular traits of intimacy, is discussed in some detail in Marrou, *op. cit.*, G. Lamb, trans. (New York: Sheed & Ward, Inc., 1956), Part I, Chap. 3.

[25] *Ibid.*, p. 17.

girls in chariots and boys on horseback paraded to the accompaniment of singing. And there were all kinds of athletic and musical competitions. At the sanctuary of Artemis Orthia, for instance, boys of ten or twelve years of age took part in two musical competitions and a "hunting" game. . . .[26]

Preparation for participation in such events was one of the important purposes of education in Sparta and in other Greek city-states. But Spartan education had a closed end—a self-centered and self-sufficient purpose that did not share the larger Greek values of goodness and justice. Philosophy and literature did not challenge Spartan thought.

In other Greek states, notably Athens, emphasis on the intellectual skills increased. By the sixth century B.C., the educational system combined an appreciation for the old aristocratic values with more practical studies. Reading, writing, and counting formed the primary school curriculum (taught by several teachers), which was preparatory to higher forms of training (received in the more traditional way).

This trend came at a time when Greek societies were expanding, making contact with the "outside" world. It thus occurred when the Greeks were both affirming vigorously their own cultural identity and reacting to external conditions and influences.

The emergence of Greek philosophical speculation about the nature of things has not been precisely defined chronologically. The eighth and seventh centuries B.C. may be said to have been the preparatory period; the sixth century marked the effulgence of new thought.[27]

Most important among these early intellectuals were the Ionian Greeks, who dwelt along the coastal and island areas of Asia Minor. Did their creativity spring from stronger tribal and ancestral traditions, or from closer contacts with older civilizations through the Hittites, the Phrygians, the Phoenicians, and the Lydians? Perhaps a combination of these factors is the explanation. Furthermore, limited economic possibilities in mountainous Greece encouraged emigration and trade, both of which served to bring an influx of new ideas. Much later, Aristotle, in his *Metaphysics,* wrote of the Greek debt to Egyptian science.

---

[26] *Ibid.*, pp. 17–18. Reprinted by permission of Sheed & Ward, Inc.

[27] Matthew T. McClure, *The Early Philosophers of Greece,* Richmond Lattimore, trans. (New York: Appleton-Century-Crofts, Inc., 1935).

The great Ionians were interested in more than social justice and artistic form. The first "philosopher," Thales (c. 624), inquired into the nature of reality; he also wrote on astronomy and was the first Greek student of geometry. Anaximander (c. 610) developed natural science—especially biology, forming a theory of biological evolution—and astronomy. Another Ionian, Xenophanes (c. 575), engaged in social criticism and theology, suggesting that a supreme God, or Mind, was the creator of all and the prime mover of all things. Pythagoras (c. 572) excelled in mathematics and music, devising a numerical scale for music that made its further development and practical use possible. He and his followers also recognized four phases of mathematics: arithmetic, geometry, astronomy, and music (much later called the *educational quadrivium*). Other sixth century philosophers who contributed to discussions of reality and existence were Parmenides (c. 540) and Anaxagoras (c. 510).

The list, of course, could be made longer, but these are the great minds of that time—they searched for truth two hundred years or more before Plato, Aristotle, and their disciples set down their doctrines.

These scientific and philosophical thinkers produced, then, new knowledge about man's nature and his environment; they reasoned, observed, and developed new theories about primary cause and ultimate order. This activity raised doubts about the validity of existing cultural traditions and about the role of religious deities and mythological teachings. Although the Greeks generally did not hold to religious dogma controlled by a separate priesthood, the new teachings did conflict with the religious norms that supported the traditional aristocratic social system and formed an integral part of the gentry's education. Conflict also occurred with the new Orphic religion, which, in the sixth century, advanced a theory of supernatural causes, a set of rites administered by a priesthood, and mystical teachings that played on initiates' imaginations. This cult did not arrest the growth of rational philosophy, however.

This period of intellectual change coincided with a time of change in the Greek social structure: economic development, commerce, and urbanization had given rise to new classes and to more wealth among landowners, manufacturers, and tradesmen. The influence of the last two groups began to spread to the political and cultural spheres. Monarchical government yielded to republican, and political and administrative reforms introduced broader public control and broke down much of the old state organization which had been based exclusively on tribal and clannish relations. Social conditions thus became more conducive to an expansion in education, which could no longer be restricted to its traditional purposes. As civic and professional needs grew, as new knowledge spread, and as the newer social classes pressed for opportunities to advance themselves, the educational sphere expanded. During the fifth and fourth centuries—the period of the flowering of Greek society—a complete educational system was worked out. As the need for educational change grew out of the new social and economic conditions of the time, the ideals of education also entered a state of flux; but the aristocratic values remained dominant. This system was not open to all Greeks, but only to citizens of the *polis,* a term which included a large body of people from various social levels.[28] In Athens, citizens numbered about 175,000 and slaves 100,000 during the fifth and fourth centuries.[29]

Content and methodology. Formal education in modern Greece trained young men for the civic and social vocations of the *polis,* particularly for service in its governing bodies: leaders groups, councils, assemblies, military establishments, and clerical personnel. In democratic Greece it was the individual who, together with his colleagues, decided in councils of state what public policies would be in matters of taxation and finance, war and peace, commerce, and social organization.

Preparation for life began at home, where the boy received from his mother and nurse knowledge of family and ancestral background, mythology, and the basic social skills. The father was the undisputed master of the household. When the boy was seven or eight years old, he was normally sent—under the care of a *paidagogos* (a kind of servant)—to primary school. There, lessons were given by several special teachers: one for the "three R's," one for music, and one for gymnastics. The student traced his letters first on

---

[28] Cf. Bury, *op. cit.,* pp. 172–78, 180–89, 332–33, 347–52; and G. Thomson, *op. cit.,* Vol. II: *The First Philosophers* (1955), Chaps. 9, 10 (this is a useful account, although the writer feels that occasionally Thomson uncritically seeks "appropriate" dogmatic citations to underscore his economic interpretation).

[29] Figures approximated from *Cambridge Ancient History,* Vol. V, p. 74; A. W. Gomme, *The Population of Athens in the Fifth and Fourth Century,* B.C. (Oxford: B. Blackwell, 1933), and "The Slave Population of Athens," *Journal of Hellenic Studies,* 66 (1946), 127–29.

waxen tablets (or sometimes on the ground), and later on paper rolls. His reading included passages from the poets (Aesop, Homer, Hesiod, and others). His knowledge of music was developed through vocal, instrumental, and dance exercises, and it was closely tied in with physical education. Lyres and flutes were his instruments. Gymnastics were organized on the playing area, the *palestra*, where individual and competitive exercises were vigorously engaged in. Religion continued to be taught, of course, both through literature and by participation in community religious events. This pattern of education, increasing in complexity with the years and merging with what is now termed *secondary education*, continued until about the boy's sixteenth birthday.[30]

In what might be called the upper secondary school, boys received further training in gymnastics and also in military matters. The earlier academic education thus formed a "general education" background for the specific training preparatory to entrance into state service (at about age eighteen). In the fourth century, students became, at the age of eighteen, *ephebes* (military cadets) and candidates for citizenship with its various responsibilities. It is not clear how extensive formal military training was, especially prior to the fourth century, but certainly athletics had become a "must" and, naturally, had some military uses. The ephebic oath, by which youths swore allegiance to their fatherland, completed this long preparatory period of schooling.

During the fifth century, this system, at first largely reserved to sons of well-to-do, aristocratic, landowning families, became more and more accessible to the masses of citizens.

Rationalistic response in educational thought to social crisis. The social liberalization of education accompanied other social and cultural changes, already alluded to, which seemed to constitute a crisis in Greek culture and a peril to its future. Critical and liberal thought had, since the time of the scientific philosophers, penetrated the arts and literature, politics, and education. Gone was the traditional unity, centered on the family and on religion, that had prevailed in Greek life and set its values and goals.

Great thinkers began to consider the state of affairs in Greece—

---

[30] Marrou, *op. cit.* (Eng. ed.), Part I, Chaps. 4, 5; Jaeger, *op. cit.*, Vol. I, Part I, Chap. 10; Woody, *op. cit.*, Chaps. 10–13. For one who desires finer details on educational practices and methods, the indicated chapters are recommended.

particularly in Athens, where a group of introspective, rationalistic philosophers dominated speculative thought for about two generations (late in the fifth century and during most of the fourth century). Led first by Socrates, then by Plato, and later by Aristotle, this group inquired deeply into the nature of truth, goodness, beauty, and justice. The inquiry generally took the form of a dialectical questioning and thinking (later called the Socratic method). This method dominated education and intellectual life well into the Christian era, when it was replaced by faith, and then was revived late in the medieval period.

One of the most influential thinkers in the field of education was Plato. In his writings (especially in his *Protagoras* and *Republic*), he advanced theoretical foundations for a new system of education. For nearly forty years, he taught these and other ideas in the *akademeia,* a grove near Athens which gave a universal name to higher studies and which endured as an educational center for nearly a thousand years. Plato believed that individual citizens should be given an education according to their endowment, and that a very few highly intelligent youths should be selected for higher, advanced studies to fit them to rule over society. These "philosopher-kings" would perennially search for truth and for knowledge of the good, found only through the contemplation of pure ideas. This knowledge would lead to an understanding of reality, of the ideal world governed by a universal Soul or Mind. The rulers, thus enlightened, would be capable only of doing what was good and right for society.

Other social classes were to receive an education suited to their calling. The guardians (army) would be educated in humanistic, civic, physical, and military studies, while the artisans-workers (including those engaged in business) would receive only the minimum education necessary for carrying on their trades. The state would control all education; marriage, family relations, and property would also be concerns of the state—not left to individual discretion.[31]

Plato railed against the popularization of knowledge and the increase of practical subject matter. These were well under way through the teaching activities of the Sophists, whom he disliked. Similar feelings are reflected in Greek literature, as in Aristopha-

---

[31] Cf. Plato's conception elaborated in B. Jowett, trans., *The Works of Plato, op. cit.,* pp. 61ff.

nes' *The Clouds,* which made a mockery of modern Greek education under the Sophists.

Aristotle followed closely Plato's social plan for education, trusting in the belief that a small elite could preserve society. But his greatest contributions to learning were in methodology (induction: proceeding from observations to generalizations) that anticipated the experimental method, in the classification of all knowledge according to subject matter, and in political science.[32] His teachings in these areas have profoundly influenced the history of Western thought and education. His creation, the syllogism, became an intellectual foundation of scholasticism in medieval times and is still valued by many thinkers.

Both Plato and Aristotle (and others close to them) approached educational problems in society from a rationalistic point of view, assuming that the goodness of society and its government depended upon the goodness of the individuals concerned. Founding his system of beliefs on a pure idealism, Plato reasoned that the perfect and virtuous man was one who had acquired perfect knowledge—and this could only be the philosopher. The highest knowledge is necessarily metaphysical—as illustrated in mathematics, in which logical proofs correct mistaken ideas derived from sensory perception. By a complete education, Plato felt, those capable of virtue could be trained to perceive and to do the highest good for society. This task of education would be its highest goal. And in order to prevent citizens from seeking selfish and sensual ends, Plato believed, property should be collectively owned.

Aristotle, too, was keenly concerned with what he considered to be education's basic function: support of a stable and good state. But he gave more attention than did his master to the individual, personal side of learning. Aristotle's keen interest in observation and analysis expressed this concern, and it led him to distinguish the various qualities, or functional aspects, of the human mind. By identifying and categorizing them, he developed the first coherent psychology, which has since been named *faculty psychology* because it recognizes distinct features of mental activity: memory, will, perception, and so on. Aristotle established a *Lyceum,* which produced

---

[32] W. S. Fowler, *The Development of Scientific Method* (Oxford: Pergamon Press, Inc., 1962), p. 18.

many scholars, teachers, and thinkers. His works and theirs were later to serve as great legacies for future European civilizations.[33]

Roman Values and Education

> Though all the world exclaim against me, I will say what I think: that single little book of the Twelve Tables . . . seems to me . . . to surpass the libraries of all the philosophers. . . .
>
> *Cicero*

Prior to its Hellenization, which began in the third century B.C., Roman society had for several centuries been shaping its own tribal and "national" cultural traditions and education. These local traits continued to distinguish Roman education, notwithstanding the tremendous influence and eventual dominance of Greek thought in the Latin world.

Prominent among the Roman's values was his practical interest— his concern for order, efficiency, and measurable results. His perennial attachment to laws handed down and reworked into the fabric of the Republic and then the Empire testifies to this practical, orderly concern. Roman educators, then, would logically give more emphasis to form, insist on specific, realizable purposes, and be less creative in their educational work than would Greek teachers. Marrou, after much study of the classical civilizations, concludes that the Romans were simply by nature less individualistic than the Greeks.[34] Whatever the explanation, evidence of the difference can certainly be found in Roman education.

Background of Roman culture and education. Rome enjoyed a maritime, peninsular position. Large mountain chains across the land approaches in the north provided natural protection from the non-Italian peoples beyond. True, the Greeks and Phoenicians colonized coastal areas on and near the peninsula, but this colonization occurred before Rome achieved dominance of Italy early in the third century B.C. Foreign colonies on Italian soil were never a threat to Rome.

Rome did not enjoy as rich a cultural heritage as did Greece with its Mycenaean forebears, although the Etruscans (still of uncertain origin) contributed some artistic and technical knowledge to the early Romans. The influence of the Greeks and other trading

---

[33] Aristotle's best-known work on public education is in his *Politics*.
[34] Marrou, *op. cit.* (Eng. ed.), pp. 229ff.

peoples outside the Italian mainland was stronger. Of Indo-European origin, Roman tribes that settled down to agriculture gradually built up an aristocratic kingship. In the sixth century B.C., monarchy yielded to a republican system controlled by a free, landowning citizenry of two social classes: patricians (large landowners) and plebeians (small landowners). In time, the patricians gained control of the Senate as well of the executive and military offices. A disenfranchised social class and slaves provided most of the physical energies that gave the aristocracy the leisure to devote to government and to cultural pursuits. Women had no rights; the male head of the household enjoyed complete authority over all its members.

This social and political system stressed certain values that marked most Roman cultural activities:

1. Freedom of landholding citizens;
2. The right to own property;
3. Strong feeling for family and religion;
4. National patriotism;
5. Legal process;
6. Agrarian interests and preferences ardently upheld by a hard-working peasantry, jealous of its customs;
7. Maternal upbringing of the young ("preschool" education).

For the educator, the role played by the mother—never by a nurse, as was often the case in Greece—in developing these basic values in her offspring was of capital importance. It also helps to explain the more practical, if conservative tradition of thinking which the Roman maintained as compared to that of the more urbane, dialectical, creative Greek. Even as late as the middle of the first century B.C., when Rome was near the height of her power and after her Hellenization, one of the greatest spokesmen for the values of Greek culture, Cicero, who was Greek-educated, felt the lasting influences of old Roman tradition: "Experience and maxims learned at home have done much more to educate me than books" (*De Re Publica*, i, xxii). The Roman's practical interests and nature thus conditioned his educational experience.

Landholding peasantry and nobility saw their civil rights largely in terms of securing property and freedom. The laws of the Republic were designed to protect these rights. Religion became a part of state service, and youths had to learn mythology as well as the household rites conducted in honor of family spirits. Religion did not pass to the control of a separate clergy, however, until the Christian period.

By that time, the emperor had become a demigod, the *pontifex maximus.*

Love and obedience in the family inspired similar qualities in the state, to which the Roman boys learned to vow a patriotism dissolved only by death: *Dulce et decorum est pro patria mori.*

Supreme loyalty to the fatherland, the nation, and the Empire, and a high sense of discipline overshadowed individual and creative values among the Romans. The old intellectual questions concerning truth, justice, goodness, and beauty were not so diligently pursued in Roman schools as they had been in Greece.

Content and methodology.   During the early Republican period (c. 500–200 B.C.), Roman boys learned to read, write, and count in primary school, and then went on to memorize the famous Twelve Tables of the law.[35] From this document they learned about procedures for settling private and public disputes over such matters as inheritance, paternal rights, and criminal punishment, as well as the ceremonials and official matters regulating public life. These laws had to be known well by all young men aspiring to public service. Roman boys also learned tribal legends and Roman history. This education program normally did not last beyond the student's sixteenth year, after which he would apprentice himself to a relative or to an acquaintance. In Rome itself it was fashionable to go to the Forum, where civic leaders could be observed firsthand. Such preparation produced an alert citizen, ready to serve in the civil and military institutions that constituted the political foundation of Roman society. A famous example of the model citizen was Cincinnatus, summoned from the plow to lead Roman armies to victory, after which he humbly resumed his farm labors. He exemplified the true citizen-soldier—the *vir bonus,* an object of Roman education.

By the end of the third century B.C., Rome was emerging as the great power in the Mediterranean and controlled many territories formerly dominated by the Greeks and Phoenicians. She had come into direct contact with their old cultures, had built an army, navy, and civil government capable of wide international responsibilities, and had developed an economic system strong enough to support these expanded activities. The Roman state and society were devel-

---

[35] Paul Monroe, *Source Book of the History of Education for the Greek and Roman Period* (New York: The Macmillan Company, 1910), pp. 334–44.

oping rapidly and many new social needs arose as a consequence of these cultural changes.

The Greek cultural influence on Roman thought, literature, and education—the Hellenization of Rome—has historically been considered to have started with the Latin translation of Homer's *Odyssey,* around 250 B.C., by the Greek slave, Andronicus. Other influences grew in the fields of oratory, medicine, agriculture, and language. Hellenization developed so rapidly that many among the Roman governing class became alarmed over the threat to traditional Roman values and the decline in their relative importance. About 150 B.C., the Senate passed a law which read, in part:

> It shall be lawful for Pomponius, the praetor, to take such measures, and make such provisions, as the good of the Republic, and the duty of his office, require, that no Philosophers or Rhetoricians be suffered at Rome.[36]

And, some fifty years later, another measure against foreign cultural influences was taken against schools where young Romans "waste their time . . . for whole days together." The law further forbade children to be given any knowledge but that which reiterated the traditions of their ancestors and it also condemned the new Greek "novelties, contrary to . . . customs." This and other measures reflected the feelings against non-Roman culture which were generated among leading Roman citizens.

But the tide of cultural change continued. About 55 B.C., Cicero could lament that "no one learns [the Twelve Tables] nowadays."[37] Roman towns in the western regions of the state, which were not founded by Greeks, imported teachers and libraries from the east. Formally, at least, Rome became a student of Greek ways. The poet Horace wrote: "At Rome I had my schooling," but it was "at classic Athens, where . . . I learnt to draw the line 'twixt right and wrong, and search for truth."[38] According to other Roman men of letters and teachers, the impact of Greek letters and literature was so great that the content of Roman education was largely transformed. Much emphasis was placed on grammer, the "Great Books," explication of text, rhetorical skills, and legal study. The art of writing received

---

[36] *Ibid.,* p. 352.
[37] Woody, *op. cit.,* p. 579.
[38] George Howe and Gustave A. Harrer, *Roman Literature in Translation* (New York: Harper & Row, Publishers, 1924), p. 373.

great attention, and teachers gave detailed instructions on how to hold the fingers and follow the lines.

Education was roughly formalized on three levels: a primary (*ludus*) school, a secondary (*grammaticus*) school, and higher schools in rhetoric, law, and architecture (and other special institutions, such as the Athenaeum in Rome). No sharp divisions existed between one level and the other, but in the secondary school, for example, a youngster mastered Greek and Latin, literature (usually studied along with grammar), history, and some rhetoric. Normally, these studies occupied a boy from about the age of twelve to the age of sixteen. If he aspired to public office or to the practice of law, he normally went on to the higher school of rhetoric. There, in addition to learning the skills of speech and logical debate, he rounded out his liberal education with instruction in arithmetic and geometry, music, astronomy, and philosophy. In these curricular sequences can be seen all of the now famous "seven liberal arts"—the trivium (grammar, rhetoric, logic) and quadrivium (arithmetic, geometry, astronomy, and music). Indeed, Roman education almost entirely duplicated the Greek in form, if not in content and purpose.

Two original contributions of Roman educators to principles of instruction and teaching are worthy of special note: the study of foreign languages and the study of contemporary literature. It was practically axiomatic that Romans would include the study of Greek in their curriculum, but that they did so established a cultural idea which European education has ever since honored (in varying degrees): a second European language (preferably Greek or Latin) is essential to a liberal education. The study of contemporary Roman poets became standard practice from the latter part of the first century B.C. on. In time, Virgil became as popular in Latin as Homer was in Greek.[39]

The outstanding sources of Roman educational thought, as well as of descriptions of Roman educational practice, are the writings of Cicero, the master orator, and Quintilian, the master teacher of rhetoric, who lived, respectively, in the first century B.C. and the first century A.D. These two men discussed in detail the education of their time, but for students of educational history, Quintilian's master work is the more instructive.[40]

---

[39] On Virgil, cf. Howe and Harrer, *op. cit.*, pp. 282ff.
[40] *The Institutio Oratoria of Quintilian*, H. E. Butler, trans. (New York: G. P. Putnam's Sons, 1920).

Quintilian's philosophy of education and his observations of educational practice in the Roman Empire are set forth in his *Institutio Oratoria*. He dealt with all the important aspects of education: organization of schools and of instruction, theories about learning, aims of education; reward-and-punishment system, standards and measurement, and problems in the psychology of education. The ultimate goal of Roman education, said Quintilian, was to produce a liberally educated person skilled in considering, judging, and speaking on the prominent issues in public life. Such a person was the orator, and the main purpose of the whole educational process was to build the orator. This task depended on a program and key ideas for its achievement. Quintilian saw the home and the primary school as the bases for all subsequent education. There children had to master reading, writing, and arithmetic. Informal methods of play were to precede formal instruction, which was not to begin until the age of seven.

As children grow, individual and maturational differences need to be considered, and also the fact that children bring cultural habits into school. Quintilian also believed that games are important for social participation and that material rewards (toys, play letters, pastries, and the like) as well as commendation need to be used to gain proper motivation. Competition and affection for the teacher, according to Quintilian, are other means for motivation. Roman pedagogues normally used the whip to get desired responses, but Quintilian frowned on corporal punishment. He also believed that schooling in groups is far superior to tutoring because of the social learning that occurs. In the teaching of languages, he maintained, Greek should precede Latin for foundational and comparative purposes. He considered language skills to be basic to success in secondary school, where training in reading, grammar, composition, speech, and music was stressed. He advocated that children's abilities be determined by testing their memories: a quick, retentive mind promised success if the disposition to work were cultivated. Formal examinations in recitation and declamation were standard practice, but Quintilian also urged that the higher schools be reserved for those who excelled in rhetoric and promised to be leaders in their chosen fields.

Quintilian's testimony on education provides much that is familiar today. He was living in the afternoon of a high civilization. The mass development of human talents had not yet become an economic necessity, but sound and acceptable ideas about education were advanced for those youngsters who were socially amenable to education.

Permeating all of Quintilian's educational thought, regardless of its specific form, was that traditional Roman concern for practical value. He was suspicious of philosophers as guardians of morality and culture; he preferred to rely on citizens trained to manage public affairs—men of character, experience, and dedication to the state. Public leadership, he felt, gave a man a good test of his worth—no armchair thinkers for him! True education and service concerned the practical affairs of society, in which cultural values had to operate.

The importance of having qualified teachers to train lawyers and statesmen encouraged the imperial Roman government to subsidize education (late first century B.C.), so that every large town soon supported a public grammar school. Beginning in the first century A.D., teachers' salaries were paid by the public treasury. Later, in the second and third centuries, teachers enjoyed exemptions from taxes, state services, and military duty. Evidence suggests that their numbers were not large, since only some five rhetoricians were publicly supported in Rome itself and normally only three in each provincial capital.[41] The principle of public support was nonetheless important, and these Roman laws endured into the medieval period. Under Emperor Constantine, various decrees (in A.D. 321, 326, 333) renewed and extended the privileges that public teachers enjoyed.

In this later period, however, Roman education and culture had ceased to be creative, and Hellenistic studies declined. We may marvel at many aspects of Rome's "modern" education system, but neither the schools nor the philosophers were instrumental in providing new solutions to social, moral, and cultural problems that weakened the Empire internally in the face of external pressures exerted by European tribal peoples migrating southward and westward. The one movement that did preach reform and re-education

---

[41] Further evidence on the limited availability of education in the later Empire is given by S. Mazzarino, "La democratizzazione della cultura nel 'Basso Impero,' " in *International Committee of Historical Sciences, XIe Congrès International des Sciences Historiques* (Stockholm, 1960), *Rapports, II* (Uppsala: Almquist & Wiksell, 1960), pp. 35–54.

—Christianity—began to influence society too late to be effective. Yet its educational record has been a significant landmark in the Western tradition.

At this point in history, therefore, Greek literary humanism and philosophy, and the Roman concern for legal and administrative arts, merged with Judeo-Christian ethical teachings to produce an educational synthesis. The early Church fathers, especially the Greek, gave it expression, although they could not guarantee its viability. At the same time, classical learning lived on.

Christian Education in the Empire

Such is our Teacher: good with justice.

Clement

From its Judaic, Near Eastern origins, the Christian sect, which was dedicated to the ministry of Jesus the Christ, gradually spread throughout the Greek and Roman provinces of the Empire. Its ethical, redeeming, and healing message was founded on a body of literature (Scriptures), tradition, and apostolic works that closely resembled the Hebrew system of religious ethics and monotheism. That both Greece and Rome, through certain of their poets and philosophers, had raised the problems of morality and ethics as basic to social health and cultural viability augured well for the new religion. As an institution, Christianity received incalculable assistance by the fourth century edicts of tolerance and state recognition as an official religion.[42] As an intellectual movement, the new religion had to compete with a system of knowledge, thought, and education that had been carefully built up for hundreds of years, and which enjoyed a literature known and loved by the social leaders of the Empire. Furthermore, Greek and Oriental mystery cults, as well as emperor worship, were popular. That Christianity could and did make headway in the classical world was, then, no mean accomplishment. The nobles and officials who managed and ruled society did not easily abandon those educational traditions that had provided their knowledge as well as their prestige. In fact, so strong

---

[42] Cf. N. H. Baynes, *Constantine the Great and the Christian Church,* in *Proceedings of the British Academy,* Vol. XV (London: Oxford University Press, 1930).

were those traditions that church leaders found it essential to master pagan culture in order to advance the cause of Christianity.[43]

The Christian churches developed instructional programs designed to introduce novitiates into the faith and to educate the clergy. Clergymen and experienced laymen offered catechumenal (instructional) lessons on the basic tenets of the religion. These learned, the believer could participate in other rites. Prospective clergymen followed a more formal and intensive program—a study of theology and practices called *catechetical education,* designed primarily for the purpose of learning to teach others (the clergy's main concern).

An outstanding Christian teacher—one through whom the educational mission of the church can be clearly seen—was Clement of Alexandria (c. A.D. 150–216), one of whose students was Origen. At the center of Clement's educational philosophy was Christ, the great teacher of mankind:

> Our pedagogue, for us, is the Holy God Jesus, the Logos who guides all humanity. . . . As for pedagogy, it is religion: it is at the same time instruction in the service of God, education toward the knowledge of truth, and good training that leads to heaven.[44]

Education, according to Clement, is moral instruction, a commitment to live daily the Christian ethic. Clement suggests that it is an extension of the classical moral teachings which helped to prepare the way for Christianity but which, with its coming, became its tributaries. ". . . Clement distinguishes a philosophy of the barbarians and one of the Greeks: this makes it easier for him to see a plan in the evolution of the human mind."[45] And for him, "The true Paideia is the Christian religion itself, . . . in its theological form. . . ."[46]

The Alexandrine teacher was well schooled in the literature and thought of Greece. Later Christian teachers, in both Roman and

---

[43] The historical accounts which follow here are largely based on the following sources: Clément d'Alexandrie, *Le Pédagogue,* Livre I, Marguerite Harl, trans. (Paris: Les Editions du Cerf, 1960); Werner Jaeger, *Early Christianity and Greek Paideia* (Cambridge, Mass.: The Belknap Press of Harvard University Press, 1961); M. L. W. Laistner, *Christianity and Pagan Culture* (Ithaca, N.Y.: Cornell University Press, 1951); and F. L. Mueller, *Histoirie de la psychologie* (Paris: Payot, 1960).

[44] Clément d'Alexandrie, *op. cit.,* pp. 207, 211.

[45] Jaeger, *Early Christianity and Greek Paideia, op. cit.,* p. 61.

[46] *Ibid.,* pp. 61–62.

Greek parts of the Empire, were also educated according to classical traditions. Tertullian, Basil the Great, John Chrysostom, Jerome, Augustine,—all had read the "Great Books." They were obliged to follow the pagan educational ideal, both because of its social dominance and because of their vocation: to refute and interpret unacceptable classical doctrines; to educate a clergy skilled in logical and rhetorical techniques of disputation and exhortation; and to establish their new erudition in a society long accustomed to learning and scholarship.

Some of the early church leaders' insights into educational problems show their almost modern understanding of psychology and of the sociocultural problems inherent in education. Although these ideas concerned mainly the educational interests of an aristocratic society based on slave labor, they nontheless merit attention.

1. *Peer influences.* Youngsters are most interested in and influenced by those things that are common to others their age. By recognizing these common interests, teachers can easily guide the group's educational activities and manipulate it in the proper or desired direction.

2. *Reward system.* Children respond much better to positive reinforcement through promises of rewards than to threats or actual physical punishment; negative action should be used very sparingly.

3. *Growth concept.* Children, like growing plants, need care at each stage of development, especially in the early years, so that later achievements (fruits) will ensue.

4. *Parental role.* Parents should read to their children, or tell them stories, so as to help edify in them the cultural values of the society.

5. *School-community relations.* Educational aims should be supported by wholesome influences in society; children need to be prevented from contacting or participating in frivolous entertainment, such as comic theater, which undermines the educational work of school and home. Attention to natural beauties, literary pursuits, and healthy recreation makes a fundamental difference in children's formative years.

6. *Physical environment.* Easy, comfortable surroundings encourage softness in a child's attitudes; austere surroundings, such as hard furniture and simple clothing, inspire firmness in character and purpose.

These early Christian ideas are in harmony with the educational theories of the high civilizations in Greece and Rome, although their ultimate purpose is religious, or confessional. Most of the leading thinkers in Christian education shared these concepts, and their importance led St. John Chrysostom to characterize the aims of education in these terms: "I am not speaking of trifles, [but of] . . . the governance of the world."

The psychological concepts underlying human behavior and forming the mental "tools" that educators employed were three traditional functions of mind: understanding (sometimes seen as the habits, mores, or meanings of a culture), or reason; will (also seen as purpose and purposeful action); and feelings (emotions, passions, and the like). These were the intangible "tools" with which teachers worked in seeking to manage behavior. St. Augustine's psychological "theory" was essentially lodged in these three concepts, and his views on the matter went unchallenged in Western Europe until the time of Aquinas—that is, for some eight hundred years.

It is clear that classical education, with its literary humanism and moral philosophy, was substantially taken over by Christian teachers and remolded into a Christian humanism in which preachers and —to some extent—laymen were schooled. Christian princes, particularly in the Eastern Empire, Byzantium, received a Christian education based on grammar, literature, rhetoric, and philosophy. Although there was no reconstruction of culture in the Empire, classical tradition lived on, as if in store for later use. Even after the collapse of the Empire in the West, schools survived in provincial towns perhaps into the eighth century. But the tribal and wandering peoples of Celtic and Germanic origin in the West, and of Slavic origin in the East, had scant use for classical learning and its schools. Until the barbaric invaders and their subjugated peoples learned to appreciate the Greco-Roman heritage, the remnants of the liberal arts in the West were taught by clergymen for ecclesiastical needs. At Byzantium, universities in Constantinople, Beirut, and a few other cities remained great centers of learning for centuries. The most dynamic factor of cultural history, however, was the intimate contact made by the newer European peoples with the older Mediterranean civilizations, which they slowly began to assimilate as their sedentary life became more developed and complex.

CHAPTER II

Medieval Culture and Education

Western Region

There is no doubt that medieval culture—insofar as learning and the arts express culture—was largely the culture of the Church. There is also no doubt that the influences of classical learning and education, as they existed in Hellenistic civilization, ceased in time. Although we cannot begin to explore the causes which brought about new cultural conditions in Europe, we can allude to the causes and briefly describe the conditions which were so little hospitable to schooling as practiced in the great Mediterranean civilizations.

In both the western and the eastern regions of the Empire, but especially in the western, the gradual encroachment by Germanic and Slavic tribes (and for a time also the Mongol Huns) on Roman frontiers led to the penetration of and, toward the end of the fourth century, to the invasion of the imperial domains. The "new" Europeans, pastoral-agricultural folk, had not long been sedentary and even as late as the seventh century had established few municipal centers for manufacture, trade, banking, or systematic administration. Tribal democracy in most areas gave rulership to elders or local monarchs. As these peoples overran the Empire, they destroyed much of existing social and political system. Some of them lived extravagantly for a time on the opulence they plundered. Imperial cities saw their populations dwindle during the fifth century; that of Rome—no longer the capital—went from about half a million to about fifty thousand. Conditions for landholding and land exploitation changed, gradually bringing about a system of independent feudal lords and vassals. These vassals were obliged to render military service in return for their fiefs. The fiefs were worked by poor peasants, many of whom were descended from Roman *colonii* and serfs as well from Germanic tribal families that settled down within the Empire. In Italy and Gaul, the situation was complex: traditional Roman settlements and their social organization existed alongside those of the invaders (as the Lombards in northern Italy). This kind of society, marked by a highly decentralized system of local laws and by tight, restrictive social relations, differed strikingly from the urban culture and liberal intellectual life developed to such a high point in Greece and Rome.[1] Who among the Celts, Germans, and Slavs would seek the literature, art, and education of classicism?

The chief patron of learning was the Church and its ecclesiastical hierarchy. A rich intellectual legacy of Christian literature and Roman administrative law placed the politically independent Roman See, as it grew in prestige, in a good position to continue in some form the classical heritage. The Church assumed most of the prerogatives in teaching formerly enjoyed by the Empire;[2] both cathedral and monastery carried on instruction, writing, bookmaking, and arts compatible with religious interests. Although the papacy itself, and its bishops, took over many temporal responsibilities, including the tenure of land and its defense, they did not extend these secular concerns into nonreligious (pagan) learning. As the pagan schools were closed down, no one in the West was able to preserve traditional learning, although some aristocratic families and monasteries used a few classical works.[3]

From the sixth century onward, medieval culture essentially rested on three concepts: priesthood, theocentricism, and monasticism. To the average layman (including, often enough, the nobility), these ideas had little meaning for his everyday culture; his tasks of producing daily food and basic goods circumscribed his cultural horizon. But for the social and cultural leaders of feudalistic Europe —the clergy and Christian rulers—those ideas had real and lasting meaning. For princes, schooling took place near the court under tutors.

The priesthood, which annointed rulers and gave holy sanction to the feudal order, taught platonically that the universe was God-centered and God-created, and in it human interests must submit to

[1] This question is discussed at length in Pierre Riché, *Education et culture dans l'Occident Barbare, VIe and VIIIe siècles, Patristica Sorbonensia No. 4.* (Paris: Editions du Seuil, 1962), especially Part I, Chap. 2.

[2] A brief account of the transfer is in Pearl Kibre, "Scholarly Privileges: Their Roman Origins and Medieval Expression," *American Historical Review,* 59 (April 1954), 543ff.

[3] P. Riché, *op. cit.,* pp. 242–44, 413–14.

divine. It was a sharp turn, historically, from the Man-centered humanism of classical times. The essential features of the new view were the condemnation of human nature in original sin, the establishment of a theory of predestination, the acceptance of revelation and faith as sources of true knowledge, and the acceptance of the universal Church as the unique path to salvation. The implications for learning and for secular culture are obvious. This rejection of immediate concern for worldly affairs, together with the primitive cultural interests of the newly settled Europeans in the West, could hardly lead to educational growth.

Christian educational institutions. Cathedral schools, organized for much the same purpose as the earlier religious schools, were found in most dioceses and were under the control of bishops. These schools gradually became the centers of learning for the clergy and, to a degree, for lay students also. Rudiments of the seven liberal arts (grammar, rhetoric, logic, arithmetic, geometry, astronomy, music) were taught there and also in monastic schools.[4] The clergy had to calculate holidays for the calendar, record the business affairs of the establishment, copy religious service books, and plan the building and decorating of their edifices. The required skills had to be mastered, often by apprenticeship.

Monastic communities, originating in the eastern regions, became popular in the later Empire as a haven from the tempestuous times and symbolized a retreat from the sinful world to the holy service of God. These ascetic groups of men, and women too, did much to preserve sources of classical learning, even though the books were never used. One of the most successful monastic orders was the Benedictine (founded about 529), whose Rule of St. Benedict became an important cultural instrument in spreading Christian learning throughout the western regions. The inspiration of this learning remained essentially religious and hostile to classical works, especially Greek; the singing of psalms replaced the study of grammar and rhetoric as intellectual armor. Conditions in the West required the clergy there to be more active, more involved in social service and practical organization, than the eastern clergy, which was still immersed in an ancient culture. The Latin clergy never reached the ascetic, withdrawn culture of the Greek (Byzantine) clergy.

---

[4] Cf. Robert Ulich, ed., *Three Thousand Years of Educational Wisdom* (Cambridge, Mass.: Harvard University Press, 1954), pp. 174 ff.

Even so, the principal aim of earthly life was so to conduct oneself as to earn a heavenly reward. The unquestioning acceptance of Christian teachings and discipline was the only correct path.

Clerical teachers, appointed by the bishop, were called *magister scholarium* (the highest rank) or *scholasticus* (the lower ranks). By the twelfth century, masters were appointed to supervise all diocesan educational activities, including the granting of degrees and the licensing of teachers.

Outstanding examples of cathedral schools were those at Chartres and Paris; monastic centers, such as York, produced the more outstanding teachers. Such schools helped support the cultural program advanced by the Carolingian house in the Frankish Empire, especially by Charlemagne (771–814). Education became an instrument of "national" policy, and a Palace School under Alcuin of York was made the model for similar schools in the Empire. The growth of a centralized state system, although shortlived, brought with it an increase in education and secular knowledge. This "renaissance" did not last, however, and intellectual progress was slow indeed during the tenth and eleventh centuries.

Late in the medieval period, in the twelfth and thirteenth centuries, the Church attempted—through papal policies—to encourage elementary education of lay parishioners by the local clergy. Although it is difficult to assess the degree of success of these measures, it appears that literacy at least was more widespread than might have been expected.[5]

The age of chivalry, of gallant knights and gracious ladies, had its own educational practices whereby pages apprenticed themselves to experienced vassals and lords to learn military skills and the arts of courtly life. Riding, dancing, manners, the use of weapons, and various sports were the main "subjects." Training culminated in a solemn ceremony in which knighthood was conferred. The culture of manor and courtly life gradually became the subject of secular writers—humanists—who created a new literary tradition.

New centers of learning. From the late eleventh century onward, a number of developments and events combined to create new values and social patterns and to challenge the traditional medieval order in Western Europe, which had been based largely on

---

[5] Cf. J. W. Thompson, *The Literacy of the Laity in the Middle Ages* (Berkeley: University of California Press, 1939).

spiritual values (as defined by the clergy). The Crusades brought masses of Europeans into contact with other regions, cultures, and institutions, and brought back intellectual influences deriving from Arabic scholarship and literary production. The revival of older Mediterranean towns and the growth of new urban centers north of the Alps brought about increased specialization in economic activities. Frequent secular-ecclesiastical disputes over properties, powers, and rights required legal and judicial services for their resolutions. There arose doctrinal disputes and discussions with the clergy; and rising monarchical states began vying with feudal lords for greater fiscal, administrative, and military power. These were the main historical changes that slowly brought about the rise of new social groups, new occupations, and new institutions.[6] They represented values that could not be accommodated within the older medieval patterns, and therefore they required the creation of new educational media—instruction methods, teachers, schools—that could produce the knowledge and skills that would be useful in the new pursuits.

Town (burgher) schools. In addition to providing apprenticeship training to youth who aspired to the mastery of a trade, townspeople in the manufacturing and trading occupations supported schools that gave instruction in reading, writing, arithmetic, religion, and some practical skills and knowledge to youth of the budding urban middle class (*bourgeoisie*). Appropriate records on these schools are scanty, but given their character and student body it seems that local languages were used instead of Latin, although the

---

[6] Materials relevant to social and cultural changes can be found in: L. Halphen, "La conquête de la Méditerranée par les européens au XIe et au XIIe siècles," *Mélanges d'historie offerts à Henri Pirenne par ses anciens élèves et ses amis à l'occasion de sa quarantième année d'enseignement à l'Université de Gand 1886–1926*, Vol. I (Brussels: Vromant & Co., 1926); S. Painter, *A History of the Middle Ages, 284–1500* (New York: Alfred A. Knopf, Inc., 1953); G. Clune, *The Medieval Gild System* (Dublin: Browne & Nolan Ltd., 1943); Pearl Kibre, "Ecclesiastical Provisions for the Support of Students in the Thirteenth Century," *Church History*, 26 (December, 1957), 307–318; G. de Lagarde, *La Naissance de l'esprit laique au déclin du moyen âge*, 6 vols. (Paris: Béatrice-Nauwelaerts, 1942–48), Vol. I, 3rd ed., 1956 and Vol. II, 2nd ed., 1958; F. Schevill, *History of Florence from the Founding of the City through the Renaissance* (New York: Harcourt, Brace and World, Inc., 1936); S. Stelling-Michaud, *L'Université de Bologne et la Pénétration des droits romain et canonique en Suisse aux XIIIe et XIVe siècles* (Geneva: Librairie E. Droz, 1955); H. Pirenne, *Medieval Cities* (Princeton, N.J.: Princeton University Press, 1925).

clergy normally was assigned the teaching role.[7] These town schools, usually supported by guild members—the "new class"—are a fine example of sociocultural change in education and suggest the subsequent cultural developments that awaited European society as it grew and prospered. Wars, famines, and plagues would take their tolls, but social life became nonetheless more complex and productive. Education had to follow suit.

Universities.[8]   The long tradition in Christian communities of teaching and licensing teachers was the main, but not the only, base for the rise of higher institutions of learning. Educated clergymen, as the guardians of theology and philosophical speculation, discussed and disputed questions of knowledge—an intellectual and scholastic pursuit that dated from the ninth century. The reform and growth of monastic orders, particularly the Benedictine, provided conditions for the emergence of clerical leaders with the leisure time necessary for learning. As a result, the forerunner of theology faculties was scholasticism, a movement led by cathedral teachers, such as Roscellinus (c. 1050–1125) and his pupil, Abelard (1079–1142), one of the most critical and scholarly clergymen of the time. Intellectual controversies stimulated research, and churchmen had sources in canon law (*corpus iuris canonici*) and commentaries— especially Gratian's *Concordio discordantium canonum*—and lay lawyers their *Corpus iuris civilis* from Roman times, to which new laws were gradually added. These sources and their glosses were greatly augmented by new materials from the classical libraries, especially the works of Aristotle—which had arrived in Europe by way of the Arabs—and, after the Crusades, from Byzantine sources. The new philosophy and methods in logic stirred controversies in theology and raised an important question about traditional learning: Could faith withstand the scrutiny of reason? These activities— together with the clergy's attempt to control educational develop-

---

[7] Thompson, *op. cit.,* p. 501.

[8] The discussion on universities is based on Hastings Rashdall, *The Universities of Europe in the Middle Ages,* new ed., 3 vols. (Oxford: Oxford University Press, 1936); Charles H. Haskins, *The Renaissance of the Twelfth Century.* (New York: Harcourt, Brace & World, Inc., 1961); Gabriel Compayre, *Abelard and the Origin and Early History of Universities* (New York: Charles Scribner's Sons, 1907); S. Stelling-Michaud, "L'Histoire des universités au moyen âge et à la Renaissance au cours des vingt-cinq dernières années," International Committee of Historical Sciences, *IXᵉ Congrès International des Sciences Historiques* (Stockholm, 1960), *Rapports, I* (Uppsala: Almquist & Wiksell, 1960), pp. 97–143.

ment—gave rise to university systems in theology and liberal arts in the latter part of the twelfth century.

Other university movements, actually older in origin, were the teaching of law and medicine. Difficulties in church-state relations and the growing rights of secular citizens encouraged the study of law and its practice. It is known that at the end of the eleventh century lectures were read in Bologna to students seeking a professional competence, and that in time both imperial and papal support was given to the granting of degrees in civil and canon law. Medicine was taught at Salerno as early as the ninth century (probably from Byzantine sources) and by the eleventh century the school's renown and influence had spread over Western Europe. Later medical facultics followed Salerno's example, but the school at Salerno itself never expanded into a university center of theology, philosophy, and liberal arts.

These university movements developed similar organizational and administrative patterns. Each originally began as a *studium,* a place where students gathered to learn under a master. In Italy, students formed a guild, or *universitas,* the right to association being an old Roman law. Teachers also formed their *universitates,* these organizations being particularly well developed north of the Alps. Hence the concept of a "university" fellowship was one of mastering the world of knowledge. As the older universities grew in importance, they sought the special status of *studium generale*—i.e., schools whose degrees made their graduates eligible to teach everywhere. Bologna, Paris, and Oxford enjoyed this privilege, which gradually was extended by papal and imperial decree to many other universities. Although thus legally sanctioned, the universities long enjoyed corporate freedom and self-government that were only much later circumscribed by the papal powers of a declining ecclesiastical hierarchy and by the increasing powers of the new monarchies.

Courses of study for students (who had to enter clerical orders) varied, but a full liberal arts course culminating in the certificate to teach (*licentia docendi*) as a "master" or *doctor philosophiae* (or *medicinae* and *juris* in case of medical and legal faculties) normally took seven years. Academic affairs were regulated through a rector, who represented both students and teachers. The granting of degrees was a prerogative of the bishop, who was also called *chancellor.*

Entry into a studium required an oral examination in Latin, the language of the intellectual elite, and a special examination in the student's chosen field. Preliminary ("determination") examinations preceded admittance to a licentiate program. The degree was earned by orally defending a written thesis.

Student bodies were identified by their national origin or country of birth, and were called *nations*. Some universities had a large number of nations; others, few. Some enjoyed excessive freedom to manage university affairs; others, only limited freedom. Although most students came from well-to-do families, the largest single social group among Swiss students at Bologna in the thirteenth century—to take only one example—was composed of middle class burgher families, a fact which suggests the growing importance of urban life for educational development.[9]

It would be difficult to overestimate the significance of the universities for European culture in general and for the development of learning and education in particular. From student benches rose new generations of intellectuals seeking rational explanations of natural and supernatural phenomena, and new sources of knowledge. The gradual rediscovery and use of classical works, including some of dubious value for Christian education (e.g., Ovid, Virgil), went hand in hand with the movement of which the university was a part. Cultural reconstruction in the West, some five or six centuries after the demise of classical education, was well underway.

Eastern Region

The Byzantine, or Eastern Empire, which survived the Western Empire by one thousand years, preserved its Greco-Roman tradition and served as a museum, a library, and a school for Europe.[10] Classical learnings merged with and helped to shape the fabrics of Church and state in the East. The Eastern Empire did not suffer the barbarian incursions to the extent that Rome did, and, in fact, in the sixth century regained much of the ground which had been lost in the West. Slavic and Bulgarian invasions, and the Arab expan-

---

[9] Cf. S. Stelling-Michaud, *L'Université de Bologne . . . , op. cit.,* pp. 115 ff.

[10] Cf. surveys on cultural history in Louis Bréheir, *La Civilisation Byzantine: L'Evolution de l'humanité,* XXXII (Paris: Editions Albin Michel, 1950); Norman Baynes and H. Moss, *Byzantium,* rev. ed. (Oxford: Oxford University Press, 1949).

sions in the seventh century, did reduce the territory of the Empire, but it remained a powerful military and political entity until late in the medieval period. This remarkable continuity was matched in the maintenance of educational and cultural institutions, where intellectual pursuits never abandoned the study of Greek literature, philosophy, history, and Roman law. Preparatory studies in grammar and rhetoric were offered throughout the long medieval period. The Christian purpose of education meant that teachings sought moral values and not the worldly wisdom or entertainment offered by pagan writings. The leaders of the Greek religious hierarchy— such as Basil the Great (c. 330–279), Gregory of Nazianzus (c. 329–89), John Chrysostom (345–407)—received a full classical education in such centers as Athens, where the university continued to function. Even after the closing of the university at Athens by Imperial decree (529) because of its strong pagan culture, other university and teaching centers carried on the tasks of secondary and higher education. The University of Constantinople (from 330), the University of Alexandria, and the University of Beirut were all outstanding; the last two, however, began to lose their Byzantine character after the Arab conquests in the seventh century. The University of Constantinople endured, with minor interruptions, until the end of the Empire, and so did the Patriarchal School. Monastic and cathedral schools for the clergy were common. Byzantine rulers, administrators, nobles, and clergymen were—on the whole—far better educated than were their counterparts in the West until the Renaissance. Patriarchs Nicephorus (eighth century) and Photius (ninth century) were liberally educated in the Greek tradition, the latter being a scholar and philosopher in his own right.[11] Emperor Constantine VII Porphyrogenetus (913–959) represented the "encyclopedic education that was given in the schools" at that time.[12] In the eleventh century, Michael Psellus reactivated the teachings of Plato and Aristotle. Many are the examples of high educational levels maintained throughout the Byzantine period. Church and state, the commercial activities of Byzantines (unsurpassed until the rise of Venice and Genoa), and pride in the traditions of Greece—all helped to support education and educators.

---

[11] Cf., e.g., his works in *Photius Bibliothèque,* René Henry, trans. (Paris: Société d'Edition "Les Belles Lettres," 1959).

[12] Bréhier, *op. cit.,* p. 467.

The programs in education were very similar to the classical tradition: primary school offered instruction in the basic skills and religion; secondary school, for children of ten to twelve, offered instruction in grammar, literature (especially Homer, whose works were studied line by line), and mathematics; and institutions of higher education offered instruction in rhetoric, logic, philosophy, science (usually astronomy), music, and mathematics. In the cathedral and monastic schools, of course, religious history, ritual, and theology were stressed. Some outstanding thinkers, hardly known in the West, were produced in Byzantium: Gregory of Sinai, Simeon "the New" of Studion Monastery, Nicetas Stethatos, Gregory Palamas,[13] and many others. It was the Greco-Roman culture of Byzantium, and particularly its religious teachings, that gave to the southern and eastern Slavs (Bulgarians, Macedonians, Serbs, Russians, Ukrainians, Belorussians) a classical heritage. The literary works of the Byzantine monks Cyril and Methodius (ninth century) gave these Slavs a common literature in Old Slavonic that brought new teachings from Greek Christian sources. They embodied a particular religious and political purpose, derived from the philosophy of history taught in Byzantium, according to which Constantinople—called the "new Rome" by the Second Ecumenical Council in 381—was the center of the Christian world and holy successor in the sequence of God's kingdoms on earth.[14] Slavic kingdoms under the influence of the Byzantine ideology (Bulgaria, Russia, Serbia) restated this historical theory in their own terms, influencing both secular and religious teachings.

There is no doubt that the educational influence of Byzantium, heir of the great Greek traditions of *paideia* and Christian orthodoxy, were basic to cultural reconstruction both in the West and in the East.

Islamic Influences

It is important to note that without the contributions of classical literature (which arrived by way of the Arabs), the medieval period and the Renaissance would have been quite different phenomena.

---

13 Cf. Jean Meyendorff, *Introduction à l'étude de Grégoire Palamas, Patristica Sorbonensia, No. 3* (Paris: Editions du Seuil).

14 An account of this idea is in William K. Medlin, *Moscow and East Rome* (Geneva: Librairie E. Droz, 1952).

Technical terms adopted by Europe from Arabic testify to this influence: *admiral, arsenal, sofa, tariff, tennis, traffic*—all are useful words and all are of Arabic origin. A survey of the great names in medieval scholarship during the eighth, ninth, and tenth centuries shows the near dominance of thinkers of Islamic culture. Even into the twelfth century, their activities strongly influenced the West. The subject content of Western education in mathematics, science, philosophy, and medicine can be shown as largely derived from Islamic (and also Hindu) sources.[15]

The relative tolerance of the Muslims (compared to their Christian adversaries) toward other cultures and religions created a favorable climate for the spread of knowledge and speculative thought. Of course, the Arabs and their allies overran the world of Hellenistic culture with its rich libraries and intellectual traditions, so that in a sense they appropriated a readymade civilization with a well-developed educational system. At least this was so in the middle and eastern Mediterranean lands. But something had to be done with this heritage, and the Muslims, in building their urban centers and religious institutions, gave much attention to schools and teachers. The Quran was specific about it: "Allah will exalt those who believe among you and those who have knowledge, to high degrees. . . . Learned people are the heirs of prophets"; and one should pray: "My God; increase me in knowledge."[16]

Out of these traditions and this contact with classical culture came some of the most learned men of the medieval age, and even of all time. A few examples must suffice to illustrate their importance for Western education. Avicenna (Ibn Sina, 980–1037), born to a Persian family at Bukhara in Central Asia (then part of the Persian Empire), was a scholar who mastered the science of medicine as it was passed down in Greek and Arabic traditions, and wrote many volumes on medicine and philosophy, reproducing Neo-

---

15 Cf. general works on Islam: H. A. Gibb, *Studies on the Civilization of Islam* (Boston: Beacon Press, 1962), G. E. von Grunebaum, *Islam* (London: Routledge & Kegan Paul, Ltd., 1961), esp. Chaps. 6, 7; DeLacy O'Leary, *Arabic Thought and Its Place in History* (London: Routledge & Kegan Paul, Ltd., 1954); Richard Walzer, *Greek into Arabic: Essays on Islamic Philosophy* (Cambridge, Mass.: Harvard University Press, 1962); Aldo Mieli, *La science arabe et son rôle dans l'évolution scientifique mondiale* (Leiden: E. J. Brill, 1938).

16 Ahmad Shalaby, *History of Muslim Education* (Beirut: Dar Alkashaf, 1954), pp. 161–62.

platonist interpretations of reality, knowledge, and being.[17] His works became known in the West and were an important source of learning—particularly his *Canon of Medicine,* which was used as a textbook.

Another Central Asian figure, Al-Farabi (c. 870–950), was of Turkish background but was educated at Khorasan and Baghdad. He studied classical philosophy and the sciences, commenting extensively on all subjects. His scientific treatises were translated into Latin and were used as sources of new knowledge in the West.[18]

Ibn Rushd, popularly known as Averroës (1126–98), was a leading Arabic thinker born and educated in Spain. He wrote on many scientific subjects, but his main influence was in philosophy, for he wrote lengthy commentaries on Greek (mainly Aristotelian) works. Translated into Latin and devoured by the Christian schoolmen, these commentaries created much controversy in religious philosophy and teaching.[19] They stressed the eternality of material forms as against a spiritual conception of creation brought about by Divine Will. The result of this controversy was a reinterpretation by the scholastic teachers, led by St. Thomas Aquinas, of traditional Christian religious philosophy. Henceforth, knowledge derived from reason and observation of nature could also be compatible with religious truth.

The great significance of this intellectual shift for the mobility of Western thought and the creation of new activity in education can hardly be overestimated. The Arabs' expansion over the classical world and in the ancient East, which led to their preservation, revival, and creation of centers of learning, served a vital purpose in the history of education—notwithstanding its sometimes destructive features. It is beyond the scope of this discussion to analyze Islam's own culture and education, however worthy of attention these are. Suffice it to say that they require better understanding so that we may know ourselves better today.

---

[17] A. F. von Mehren, "La philosophie d'Avicenne," *Le Muséon, Revue des sciences et des lettres,* Vol. I–1 (1882), pp. 389–409; and "Les rapports de la philosophie d'Avicenne avec l'Islam," *Ibid.,* Vol. 2–1 (1883), pp. 460–74.

[18] Cf. I. Madkour, *La place d'Al-Farabi dans l'école philosophique musulmane* (Paris: A. Maisonneuve, 1934).

[19] Haskins, *op. cit.,* pp. 346 ff.

CHAPTER III

Changes in Education through the Renaissance and the Reformation

Humanism South and North of the Alps

> To know by heart only is not to know at all.
>
> *Montaigne*

The transition from medieval, ascetic-religious culture to what tradition terms the Renaissance, with its new emphasis on human interests and values, was not a sudden social and cultural outburst. The gradual growth in new social institutions and intellectual developments emerging from human conflicts, adjustments, or creativity had—over the centuries—produced a European society that could not accommodate its needs and interests within a feudal and ecclesiastical framework. The rise of urban commercial centers, the emergence of princely monarchical states, the conflicts between secular and clerical powers, the effects of Arabic and Byzantine influences, the changes in theories of knowledge from faith toward reason and naturalism, the growth of scholarship in universities—all these important developments created a mass of new cultural elements with which man had to be concerned in educating and training himself. The mass of people, of course, made up of enserfed peasantry, still provided the labor to produce food and necessities for those who managed society.

The expansion of social vocations and cultural pursuits demanded a new kind of education. The humanist spirit of the times, both in Italy and in the northern countries, best expresses the general aims and values of the new schools.[1] Scholastic education, together with

---

[1] On humanism and education, the following sources are useful: Frederick Eby, *The Development of Modern Education,* 2nd ed. (Englewood Cliffs, N.J.: Prentice-Hall, Inc., 1952); I. L. Kandel, *History of Secondary Education* (Boston: Houghton Mifflin Company, 1930); Crane Brinton, *The Shaping of the Modern Mind* (New York: The New American Library, 1953); P. O. Kristeller, *The Classics and Renaissance Thought* (Cambridge, Mass.: Harvard University Press, 1955); Erich Auerbach, *Dante: Poet of the Secular World,* R. Manheim, trans. (Chicago: The University of Chicago Press, 1961).

the recovery of classical learning, produced in time a critical attitude toward social institutions and cultural traditions. More and more, man became the center of thought and he began to regard his stay on earth as something more than a trial of deprivation and suffering preparatory to either a heavenly or an infernal reward. New religious thought, inspired by Neoplatonic philosophy, turned away from the cold logic of scholasticism and toward the ideal, the good.

In secular society, the ancient literature and teaching goals of the non-Christian Greco-Roman world, which had been steadily creeping into intellectual life since the eleventh and twelfth centuries, came into vogue. Added to this heritage were the vernacular, romantic poetry and stories of such writers as Andreas Capellanus, Dante, Wolfram von Eschenbach, Chaucer, and a host of others. On the religious side, a series of independent thinkers—Wycliffe, Huss, Savonarola, Marsiglio of Padua, William of Ockham—and such movements as the Waldensians, Albigensians, and Lollards broke the spiritual unity of Christendom and gave religious support to nationalistic tendencies in Europe. Although the Roman Church attempted to adjust its teachings through doctrinal change, censorship, and harsh punishments, the sociocultural changes across Europe produced educational practices that aimed to develop nonecclesiastical values. The new, humanist values pertained to physical grace and beauty, artistic enjoyment, material wealth, literary education, political skills, and the cultivation of human tastes in general. Of course, the more religion-oriented humanists—especially in the countries north of the Alps—stressed Christian simplicity, purity, and idealism in addition to some of the other values. They also sought to expose the corruption of worldly clergymen.

South of the alps.   In Italy, the assimilation of Germanic tribes into native Italian society and culture had long since taken place. Especially in the towns of central and northern Italy, well-to-do families in Florence, Venice, Genoa, and Padua, as well as the nobility of the rural estates, became patrons of the arts and of education. University studies in Italy had grown more out of legal and medical traditions than from theological pursuits, and this characteristic was shared by humanism and education in general. Italian society was essentially less concerned with reforming religious values than with pursuing secular humanistic learning.

Schools or academies for the education of the social elite were operated privately by such humanists as Pietro Vergerio (1340–1420), Battista Guarino da Verona (1374–1460), and Vittorino da Feltre (1378–1446). They also wrote treatises on education that were long influential in all Europe. Other humanists, such as Aeneas Sylvius (later to become Pope Pius II), contributed to educational thought. His *Education of Children* (1451), which was based on Roman ideas, advocated teaching the classics, mathematics, and other practical subjects as well as religion. The great Leonardo da Vinci (1452–1519) more vigorously opposed medieval traditions by insisting that science must be "born of experiment."

One of the best accounts of the humanist school in Italy is that left by Vittorino, at Mantua. During the first half of the fifteenth century, he prepared himself for and then developed an academy — a boarding school for boys—that taught the ancient seven liberal arts and religion.[2] Three principal aims guided its pedagogical work: physical development, intellectual development, and character development. Methods of teaching the classical curriculum were directed toward achieving these aims. This curriculum embraced Latin and Latin literature, Greek and Greek literature, grammar, rhetoric, logic (not intensive), mathematics, astronomy, music and drawing, ancient history and philosophy, nature studies, and physical-military exercises. This study program itself is evidence of the humanists' knowledge of classical Greco-Roman culture. But by this time the humanists were also well acquainted with Cicero's and Quintilian's works on education. Vittorino insisted that teachers consider the differences among children, and adjust their teaching methods accordingly. If a lad learned more slowly or in a manner different from that normally followed, the teacher should vary the lesson, make it more simple, illustrate, and so on. If the student was to be successful, his best talents would have to be discovered through teaching. Games and playthings were used for younger children (some girls were included)—such things as little letter cards of different colors. As in classical education, much work went into grammar and speaking, the mastery of which was considered a sound basis for success in other disciplines and an excellent mental exercise.

This type of humanist school, then, might well be characterized

---

[2] William H. Woodward, *Vittorino da Feltre and Other Humanist Educators* (Cambridge: Cambridge University Press, 1912).

as having both a literary and passive pedagogical approach, and an active—to some extent "behavioristic"—pedagogy. Perhaps this last qualifier is a bit ambitious for the fifteenth century, but at least some of the ingredients of sense realism were present. Teacher-pupil relationships ideally were understanding, if not tender. Reward and punishment came by way of moderate praise and occasional use of the rod. Classes were kept as small as possible so as to allow ample attention to individual needs. Subject-matter lessons were worked out in detail, with great care taken with reading and grammar. Children usually entered the school between the ages of five and ten— enough variation in terms of today's knowledge to make some difference!

Well-directed academies, such as the one described above, ranked close to universities at that time—in fact, Vittorino considered acquiring university status. The academy at Florence, where the Byzantine scholar Chrysoloras (c. 1350–1415) taught Greek philosophy, was a great intellectual center that did not, however, enjoy the rights of a *studium generale* (see p. 41). And so it was with many other Italian humanistic schools.

North of the alps.   The main problem in discussing humanistic education in West, Central, or East Europe is, of course, the greater variety of cultural and ethnic elements that differentiate educational thought and institutions. Arbitrary selection is the only path to take.

One generalization that is perhaps safe to make is that the religious movement was a leading force in northern humanism. In France, the strong religious reform sentiments of the sixteenth and seventeenth centuries had their historical roots in the French leadership in theology and philosophy which began in medieval times. In Germany and England, too, religious matters provided the chief impetus for cultural and educational reform. Similar values could be identified in Bohemia-Moravia, Poland, and Russia. Underlying these religious movements were new social energies and political interests. In this sense, the situation in the north resembled that in Italy. The rising commercial towns, especially in the Hanseatic League (from the thirteenth to the seventeenth centuries), played no small part in the social transformations that sought new cultural expression.

Renewed interest in Biblical studies brought new translations of Holy Scripture and, with them, intensive reading of early Christian

and Hebrew literature. Alexander Hegius (1433–98), Desiderius
Erasmus (1466–1536), John Colet (1467?–1519), Johann Reuchlin (1455–1522), Johannes Wessel (1420–89), and Guillaume
Budé (1467–1540) are some of the more prominent men of the
northern Renaissance who worked actively in educational affairs.
All were well educated in the classics and acquainted with Italian
humanism; they put their knowledge and skills to work at reforms
that were clearly directed to new religious thought and to the social
groups espousing it.

One of the most influential movements in education, and one
which predated the activities of these humanists, was the "Brethren
of the Common Life." Organized in the latter part of the fourteenth
century, the group sought to improve religious practices in the
Netherlands and northern Germany, and to make available teachers
and teachings among the people. Its followers became teachers in
the town or burgher schools, and they condemned much of the stiff
and somewhat sterile educational practices traditionally followed by
the clergy. In religion, they called for a return to Scripture and pa-
tristic writings. In Germany the "Rhineland Mystics" also sought a
pure Christianity.

As did the Italian educators, the trans-Alpine teachers nearly
abandoned logic to stress literature and, in some schools, religious
ethics. The original Greek and Latin texts were used, and some comparative studies were undertaken by recourse to the original Hebrew
in religious exegesis. The aims of this education were to produce
good men, fine writers and speakers, and persons well acquainted
with the world about them. In the main, these humanists were less
concerned with developing physical charms and artistic tastes than
with stressing ethical values. Such was the kind of educational "product" that historical conditions favored. Both northern and southern
humanisms struggled hard to have the Latin of Cicero prevail in
learning, teaching, and expression. The great moral and ethical lessons of classical literature, as well as its humorous and sometimes
immoral themes, were claimed to teach eternal cultural values to be
experienced by the well-educated.[3] Also, the study of Latin would
equip the Christian to avail himself of the Church's redemptive mission. The great stress (which in hindsight appears excessive) on

---

[3] Cf. the Italian viewpoint in F. Le Van Baumer, *Main Currents of Western
Thought* (New York: Alfred A. Knopf, Inc., 1952), p. 138.

teaching classical Latin can be largely explained by the fact that the corpus of classical learning had been passed on in Latin manuscripts or in Latin translations from Greek and Arabic. Under ecclesiastical control, education and learning had been conducted in Latin. It was the language of the elite, and its possession opened to one the doors of intellectual privilege, education, and the professions. (Its function has been likened to that of initiatory rites required in discriminating social systems.[4])

The new European culture and its educational expression had drawn a great deal, then, from its forerunners. Is it correct to see in this relationship a similarity to that which existed between classical Greece (and, to some extent, Hellenistic Rome) and the Mycenaean civilization of Greece, whose heroes Homer idealized? The similar time intervals are suggestive, as are the respective sociocultural progressions from primitive social orders to highly differentiated and complex structures. The course of educational changes in each of the two periods is likewise very similar.

Useful illustrations of northern humanistic schools during the period here considered are those of John Colet in England and of Johannes Sturm at Strasbourg. Both had extensive influence on educational history.

Colet, educated at Oxford, Paris, and Italian law schools, became Dean of St. Paul's Cathedral School in 1509. He appointed William Lily, the classical grammarian, as his first headmaster. Under the reforming management of Colet, Lily produced a new Latin grammar which was much more practical than its predecessors (it later became known as the *Eton Latin Grammar* and was still in use in the nineteenth century). Colet opposed the scholastic methods which governed pedagogy, and his liberal ideas brought many changes. He insisted on the use of English in some lessons, especially religious, and used modern authors, such as Erasmus, as well as the ancients. Excerpts from the school's *Statutes* illustrate these points in the English of the day:

> . . . I will the Chyldren lerne ffirst aboue all the Cathechyzon in Englysh and after the accidence that I made or sum other yf eny be better to the purpose to induce chyldren more spedely to laten

---

[4] Cf. Walter J. Ong, "Latin Language Study as a Renaissance Puberty Rite," in *Education and Culture,* George D. Spindler, ed. (New York: Holt, Rinehart & Winston, Inc., 1963), pp. 444–66.

spech An thanne Institutum Christiani homines which that lernyd Erasmus made at my request and the boke called Copia of the same Erasmus And thenne other auctours Christian as lactancius prudentius and proba and sedulius and Juuencus and Baptista Mantuanus and suche other as shalby thought convenyent and moste to purpose vnto the true laten spech all barbary all corrupcion all laten adulterate which ignorant blynde folis brought into this worlde and with the same hath distayned and poysenyd the olde spech and the varay Romayne tong which in the tyme of Tully and Salust and Virgill and Terence was vsid, whiche also seint Jerome and seint ambrose and seint Austin and many hooly doctors lernyd in theyr tymes. . . .[5]

In Colet's school, as in most other English humanistic grammar schools, the Latin of Cicero and the poetry of Virgil held first rank in the literary curriculum. Throughout Europe, "Ciceronianism" had been established, its role not unlike that of the Homeric poems in Greek education.

This phenomenon can also be seen in Sturm's college at Strasbourg from about 1537, where he aimed above all to have students master the "purity and elegance of diction."[6] After teaching classics at the University of Paris, where Peter Ramus was one of his students, Sturm became a Protestant and went to Strasbourg to teach. He established a college, based on classical languages and literature, which became a model for reformist leaders in education.[7] The program began with reading and writing in Latin, then went into Ciceronian literature and some other authors (Virgil, Demosthenes, Plautus, Terence, Homer, and so on) whose works had value for rhetorical purposes. The emphasis on grammar, logic, rhetoric, ethics, and history, to the near exclusion of other liberal arts, was overwhelming. It seems, however, to have been in keeping with the spirit of religious reformation, antagonistic toward other areas of secular and practical knowledge as such. In fact, Sturm's program had much influence on both Lutheran and Calvinistic Europe.

Other brands of humanistic thought in education, particularly in sixteenth-century France, deserve some attention in view of their pertinence to the cultural needs of the emerging middle class and their later use in the reconstruction of educational theory. The most

---

[5] Paul Monroe, *A Textbook in the History of Education* (New York: The Macmillan Company, 1938), p. 394.

[6] Eby, *op. cit.*, p. 91.

[7] Kandel, *op. cit.*, pp. 87–88.

interesting examples are Montaigne, Rabelais, and Vives (a Spaniard who lived in England).

A monk, physician, and writer, François Rabelais (died 1553) used his clever head and hand to heap ridicule upon the old, sterile, and coarse culture of medieval scholasticism. His fictitious characters, Gargantua and Pantagruel, are depicted so as to satirize the meaningless mass of learning that pedagogical tradition required young men to commit to memory. Almost a walking encyclopedia himself, Rabelais saw an intellectual wasteland blighting educational pursuits, and a gross failure to relate educational needs to the interests of society. This was no doubt the meaning of Gargantua's second educational experience, whereby he acquired "real" knowledge (including history), engaged in physical exercises, pursued practical sciences, and generally went about his studies in an enjoyable, relaxed manner. His religious studies concentrated on the Bible itself, where he learned to hope in a good God whose creation was wonderful, not a condemned place fraught with sorrows. Gargantua studied practical arts where they were practiced, from stonecutters, woodcarvers, goldsmiths, furniture makers, and the like. Education, suggested Rabelais, should relate to life and make use of the energies, disposition, and environment of children, rather than crushing these into a medieval mold. The creative climate and urban social growth that marked the sixteenth century would have been, it seems, conducive to such ideas in education.

Speaking in a similar vein, Michel de Montaigne (1533–1592) studied law and read widely in classical culture before giving serious attention to humanistic education. Less satirical and more positive than Rabelais, Montaigne saw the need for a reconstruction of education. He did not have in mind, however, large classrooms of children, but rather the upbringing and instruction of youngsters by tutors, according to the fashion of his time and society. Although his family descended from the middle class, they had acquired wealth and a title. Montaigne was thus well acquainted with the values and habits of the bourgeoisie as well as with those of the aristocracy. For a few years he served at the courts of Henry III and Henry IV.

As a humanist thinker and observer, Montaigne developed a modern concept of the educational process. As Locke would later, he refused to regard Greek and Roman literature as the repository of every truth, and he rejected the reading of Latin as a goal of education. "History is my chief study," he said,[8] because it brings one new understandings through the experiences of others. He saw similar values in novels and in poetry. But he opposed any memoriter learning: "To know by heart only is not to know at all."[9] He was just as opposed to the substitution of logic and the rhetorical arts for real knowledge of one's subject.

Montaigne encouraged self-knowledge and humility. This attitude, plus the teacher's knowledge of the individual pupil, allows the student's education to be developed in his best interests, not shaped in accordance with any preconceived notions. Such individualized instruction would be a far cry from the tutorial practices common in his day. It would also build character rather than pompous conformity to externally determined values.

From Aristotle's writings and from his own personal childhood experiences, Montaigne acquired an appreciation for habit and for operational phases of learning. He learned Latin by speaking it (this was Erasmus' position); and he pointed out how well peasants and craftsmen accomplish their tasks and exercise wisdom without having to go through schooling, because they learn by example and habit. In fact, a peasant woman used to carrying a small calf in her arms pursued the habit so that when the calf was full-grown, she could still carry it about!

Montaigne wanted education to build a strong bond between learning and doing, between the intellectual idea and its practical implementation. Speculative knowledge divorced from practical affairs is of no value, he maintained, nor is the amassing of facts without regard to their meaning or to their use in making decisions. According to Montaigne, judgment is better than erudition.

To reach his educational values, he would chart new paths for children. These would include much physical activity, including games, to develop muscle skills, coordination, and over-all comprehension. Bodily exposures to heat, cold, and nature would be a part of education and lead to physical conditioning. Learning should be a pleasant experience, on the whole, not one based on dread of punishment (Montaigne deplored beating). Teachers should make

<hr>

[8] Montaigne, *The Education of Children*, L. E. Rector, trans. (New York: Appleton-Century-Crofts, Inc., 1899), pp. 20, 42–43, 151 ff.
[9] *Ibid.*, p. 33.

use of the joyful and optimistic nature of children; love ought to be the basis of their relationship. Children need to see practical outcomes of things learned; as far as is possible, subject matter should be related to life and to actual experiences. Finally, moral education should be sought through development of a character based on humility, honesty, and goodness.

Like Rabelais, Montaigne was somewhat of a voice in the wilderness, but he was less bothered by censure than was the good doctor. Although he did not favor experimental science, he did advocate activating the senses and using careful observation in education. His aims, values, and methodology classify him as different from the traditional humanist steeped in literary learning; he was an educational thinker close to sense realism. Montaigne reached this position without personal teaching experience and without careful, prolonged observation of schools. But his critical thinking about education proved to be most fruitful.

Juan Vives (1492–1540), a native of Spain, received his early education there and then went on to the University of Paris. He spent some years studying and tutoring in England, until he incurred the displeasure of Henry VIII, who sent him off to the Continent. He wrote his outstanding works on education and social problems while in England. In terms of his real concern for the actions and behavior of the human mind, Vives was perhaps the most original educational thinker of the Renaissance. He asked questions about mental actions and feelings, and how these apply to learning.[10] As a royal tutor of princesses, he also considered women's education, which became a topic of discussion in the sixteenth century. Vives was led to the conclusion that the mind learns inductively, and that this fact had clear implications for teaching and learning. It was essential to use the senses, after which reflection would make meaning out of the experience. Vives was far ahead of his time.

All these educational thinkers, and many more, were indebted to the learning and writing of the most accomplished intellect of their age: Erasmus. Although he concerned himself with pedagogy only in passing, Erasmus' keen observations and remarks on the need for reform in education rank him as one of the most creative thinkers in

---

[10] F. L. Mueller, *Histoire de la psychologie* (Paris: Payot, 1960), p. 158; Eby, *op. cit.*, pp. 50 ff.; James Mulhern, *A History of Education*, 2nd ed. (New York: The Ronald Press Company, 1959), p. 356.

the history of the subject. Perhaps one of his most telling attitudes was that toward Latin, which he insisted be taught by the natural method rather than by years of drilling on words and memorizing texts. Most modern humanists still do not believe him.

The literary and artistic flowering of European society did not fail to bring women onto the scene in new roles. The very attention given to artistic graces helped to enhance this new interest, and with the revival of pre-Christian romantic poetry, the place of women in social life was further idealized.[11] Girls were sometimes admitted as students, along with their brothers, in the humanistic academies. As court life increased in importance and changed in content—becoming, as it were, a center of musical, literary, and decorative interests—the hand and intellect of the ladies were solicited more and more. It became necessary, indeed, that women—such as Isabella d'Este Gonzaga and her later imitators, who created an enviable place in the salons where culture and feminine charms mixed—receive an education fitting such roles. It would take many generations, however, for women of less than courtly rank to win access to education and to be considered fit for parlor life alongside their men.

Reformation Educational Thought

I maintain that the civil authorities are under obligation to compel the people to send their children to school. . . .

Luther

The educational ideas that marked the Reformation, as well as the Reformation itself, were essentially new expressions of a process that had been going on for hundreds of years. Certainly there occurred something new and even revolutionary, and the great men of the sixteenth century were its principal artisans. The way in which they acted on educational problems, and especially the new relationships which developed between school and society—are of utmost importance.

Martin Luther (1485–1546), the peasant monk educated at the University of Erfurt in the scholastic tradition, rose up in defiance of the culture that demanded that as a child he be frequently

---

[11] On Italian women, in particular, see the sketch in Edith Sichel, *The Renaissance* (London: Butterworth & Co. [Publishers], Ltd., 1940), pp. 129 ff.; and some vivid descriptions in *The Horizon Book of the Renaissance* (New York: The American Heritage Publishing Co., 1961), pp. 345 ff.

whipped and that as a Christian he bow to a worldly church. He was a vigorous exponent of reactivating true Christian culture with its liberating and ennobling mission,[12] and he meant for the school to be an active agent in this development. His was a popular revolt, aimed—at least in its early phases—at benefitting the people at large. If the earlier humanists had a vision of well-to-do citizens trained in the service of the city-state or of the royal court, Luther and his followers envisioned a mass Christian citizenry educated for service to God and country. This change put the emphasis on *individual* man as a socially responsible Christian—hence the difference from the more secular humanist concept. This trend is clear in Calvinism also. Both movements found support among the emerging middle classes, who sought an end to feudal privileges and restrictions on trade and an end to an infamous ecclesiastical tax system controlled from a distant papal throne that inspired little if any religious sentiment. In this struggle for change, local rulers and city magistrates often made common cause with the religious reformers. Luther's sharp tongue, which lashed out with phrases ridiculing cloisters for "blockheads" or "servile flatterers of the pope," and Calvin's careful logic provided the necessary intellectual leadership to weld together these various interests.

Education in Lutheran Germany.   Although Luther favored many social changes, he stressed the need for re-educating the people before these could be carried out successfully. On the basis of Scripture, he appealed to German officialdom to provide funds and administration for education.[13] For the individual to acquire religion, it was essential that he read the Bible—and the most direct way to this end was to place that book in the hands of all believers in their *own* tongue and to educate them to read it. Obviously, schools for primary education were needed in great numbers. This

---

12 Cf. Edgar N. Johnson, *An Introduction to the History of the Western Tradition,* Vol. II (Boston: Ginn & Company, 1959), 73 ff. Other suggestions are Karl Adam, *The Roots of the Reformation* (New York: Sheed & Ward, 1951); Roland H. Bainton, *Here I Stand: A Life of Martin Luther* (New York: The New American Library, 1955); Basil Hall, *John Calvin* (London: Wyman & Sons, Ltd., 1956); John T. McNeill, *The History and Character of Calvinism* (New York: The Oxford University Press, Inc., 1954); R. Schwickerath, *Jesuit Education: Its History and Principles* (St. Louis: B. Herder, 1904); Allan P. Farrell, *The Jesuit Code of Liberal Education* (Milwaukee: Bruce Publishing Co., 1938).

13 Cf. his 1524 appeal to the magistrates in R. Ulich, *Three Thousand Years of Educational Wisdom* (Cambridge, Mass.: Harvard University Press, 1954), pp. 218–38.

Lutheran requirement was the most important educational develop- ·
ment in European history since ancient times. Its portentous significance was that the language of spiritual culture was the individual's
own tongue, and that in time this identification would spread to
other elements of culture. The secularization of knowledge by the
displacement of Latin advanced by a great leap. This is not to suggest that the native languages had not been used in schools before;
they had, in the many town schools supported by the rising middle
class who needed a more practical learning for their children in
order that they might participate in the family and guild economies.
But the cultural implications of Luther's educational policy were
much broader, for they foreshadowed an extensive socialization
process for whole populations which adhered to the reform movement. This adherence brought with it an entirely new approach to
culture—a culture based on national languages and national traditions. The universality of Latin and, in large measure, of the classical
civilization as well as the religious system it represented became a
matter of history. The eventual dominance of the English, French,
German, Czech, Polish, and Russian languages in European literature could be seen in the light of this and subsequent similar reforms.
Luther went so far as to boast that reading German precluded the
study of the commentaries of the Church Fathers on Biblical matters. This attitude helps in part to explain the relative lack of attention by the Lutherans to university studies which, for this and a ·
number of other reasons, fell significantly in quality during the sixteenth and seventeenth centuries.

Luther insisted that parents put their children, boys and girls,
into schools, for no less than an hour or two every day. Education,
correctly managed, would make useful and efficient citizens. Public
authorities, as well as ecclesiastical, ought to value education, therefore, and Luther sought financial and administrative support from
the state. He could not look to the established church he had just
left, so he placed both his reform and its school under the protection
of the secular authorities. His view on the subject was unequivocal:

> I maintain that the civil authorities are under obligation to send
> their children to school, especially such as are promising. . . . If the
> government can compel such citizens as are fit for military service to
> bear spear and rifle, to mount ramparts, and perform other martial
> duties in time of war; how much has it a right to compel the people

to send their children to school, because in this case we are warring with the Devil. . . . The Turk does differently, and takes every third child in his Empire to educate for whatever he pleases.[14]

This decision was a crucial one, for it raised the vital question of the future relations of church and state, and the problem of spiritual independence. Indeed, Luther had no other source of support than the local civil authorities once he abandoned the institutional framework of a universal church whose officials wielded temporal powers as well as ultimate spiritual sanctions. The reform had to find a social base. (Calvin, too, would have to find a solution, and he worked out a different arrangement.)

For mass education, the catechism was translated into German, and a German hymnbook published. Aesop's fables also appeared in the native tongue. The study of arithmetic, history, and music was advocated. Church staffs, pastors, and sextons were obliged to conduct schooling, since no other teachers were available for these new tasks. State and church could pass ordinances on obligatory education, but they could not create teachers. This urgent need would, in time, lead to formal teacher training schools.

One of Luthers trusted and able supporters, Philip Melanchthon (1497–1560), a relative of Reuchlin, served as his educational adviser. On the basis of his erudition and knowledge of German conditions, Melanchthon worked out plans for establishing secondary schools and universities to replace traditional institutions and to give the reform an intellectual basis. The German gymnasium, under his influence, developed a curriculum and regimen very similar to that of Sturm's academy. Latin was taught as the queen of tongues, German and other languages being expressly forbidden. Ciceronian style and the ethics of classical literature reigned supreme. Melanchthon himself had no interest in the popular schools where German and practical subjects were taught; his concern was for schools that would educate German social leaders—princely and civil authorities, pastors, and teachers. At the higher level, new universities (at Marburg, Königsberg, Jena, Helmstedt) were created, and older ones (at Wittenberg, Tübingen, Leipzig, Frankfort, Greifswald, Rostock, and Heidelberg) were reformed.[15]

---

14 Eby, *op. cit.*, p. 73.
15 *Ibid.*, p. 88.

Calvinist concepts of education.   The French reform movement and its educational expressions were destined to have more influence outside France than in their own country. But because of its origin and leadership, the movement was predominantly French in conception and character. This means it was both more theological and more intellectual than the Protestant movements elsewhere, especially in Lutheran Germany. Much credit for these differences goes to its leader, Jean Calvin (1509–64), well trained in law, philosophy, theology, and the classics. Although nourished in scholasticism and its Aristotelian logic, he was also influenced by the idealism of Neoplatonic thinkers such as Peter Ramus, who soundly refuted the foundations of scholastic knowledge. One of the great teachers of the time, Mathurin Corderius, was his mentor in Paris. Corderius stimulated individual thought and inquiry and a taste for critical scholarship. Calvin acquired many pedagogical ideas at Strasbourg, where he observed the gymnasium of Sturm. At Basel, Switzerland, he wrote his great religious and theological treatise, *Institution de la religion Chrétienne* (1536, in Latin; 1541, in French).

As a cultural goal, Calvin sought to restore theology as the queen of disciplines in Christian education. To him, Latin scholasticism had subverted divine studies to empty exercises in logic. The social content of his reform consisted of making the individual responsible for his conduct and his spiritual achievement, and reaching the masses by using the mother tongue to teach religious fundamentals and the Bible. The former idea appealed especially to the rising middle class, which depended not on landed estates for their wealth and standing, but rather on individual merit, hard work, thrift, accumulation of capital, and initiative—qualities that had, over the centuries, been nurtured in urban merchant families. Just as the Athenians had boasted, in the fifth century B.C., that a man's success is the proof of his worth, so the Calvinists would say that proof of a man's salvation and election lay in his success.

In order to realize these values and to advance the religious reform, a system of schools was deemed necessary. The social and political conditions whereby education and religion were promoted at Geneva, the French-speaking city that received Calvin as a reformer, merit special attention because of their enduring significance and their differences from the Lutheran schools.

When Calvin was first called to preach reform in Geneva, the elected city council had already established the principle of local, independent, representative government. In 1536, the council, exercising the executive power invested in it, invited Calvin to Geneva. The government, ruling by virtue of a contract with the governed, had committed the city-state to a church program based on religious and educational reforms. Later Calvin made broad demands on the government so that he might depend on civil authority in carrying out his reforms. Concessions were made, but still Calvin was an appointed head of church, responsible to an elected government. Church and state governed in mutual agreement, establishing a state religion, a committee for the supervision of public morals and religious orthodoxy (the consistory), and schools. Both the civil and the clerical administrations, therefore, had jurisdiction over the education and upbringing of youth, and the schools served a specific community function. Community consent and participation in education were thus uniquely provided for in the institutional formula worked out by Calvin at Geneva. In terms of orderly and responsible cultural change, the arrangement was a dynamic innovation in Western social thought and practice.

The school statute of 1559 required that teachers selected for the new college appear before "the members of the Council in order to be approved and confirmed, according to their good pleasure."[16] Likewise the school principal (*le principal*) received appointment at the discretion of the city council and had to meet the religious requirements of the church. He should be, according to the statute, "of a kindly spirit and not rude and harsh, so that he may give a good example to his students all his life and bear gently the vexations of his task."[17] A system of four school districts was set up under the college (a secondary school similar to Sturm's gymnasium), whose curriculum culminated in theology and actually seems to have reached an academic level comparable to that of a university. The school had a total of seven classes (Sturm's had ten), in each of which the students were divided into groups of ten without attention to chronological age or home origin. Each group was headed by

[16] S. Stelling-Michaud, *Le Livre du recteur de l'Académie de Genève (1559–1878)*, Vol. I: *Le Texte, "Travaux d'humanisme et renaissance"*, XXXIII (Geneva: Librairie E. Droz, 1959), p. 67. For the idea of government in Geneva in the sixteenth century, see E. Choisy, *La théocratie à Genève au temps de Calvin* (Geneva: M. Reymond & Cie, 1897).

[17] Stelling-Michaud, *op. cit.*, p. 68.

a member of that group (a kind of monitor). Instruction began with a Latin-French *ABC* book, reading, writing, and Latin. In the last level (grades were numbered from seven to one), studies concerned logic, rhetoric, and literary analysis of texts in Cicero, Demosthenes, Homer, and Virgil. Earlier subjects included ancient history, literature, philosophy, theology, elements of physical science, French, and, of course, the classical languages (Greek, Latin, and Hebrew). The inclusion of two "modern" subjects, besides reformed religious teachings, is small but encouraging evidence that education was attentive to certain practical needs and to changing values. An annual examination, written in French, determined whether the student merited advancement to the next class.[18]

The entire school regimen and atmosphere exhibited education's main purpose: to edify the new religion and to cause its precepts to reign in social life. The students would one day be leaders in their respective communities, which extended from Geneva to all corners of the European continent. It is said that some nine hundred students were enrolled during the college's first year, although the registration lists of the Rector's book show only 162 names.[19]

Calvin's great efforts, and the collaboration of the civil authorities, made his cultural and educational reform one of the leading examples of its kind in all of Europe. Thus, although he had not found in his own homeland a social foundation for the reform, Calvin and Calvinism won vigorous support in some of the leading countries (in terms of social and economic progress) of Europe, such as Holland, England, Scotland, Switzerland, Hungary, and Poland. In North America, Dutch and English colonists would bring Calvinism as the cultural foundation of their new life and society. In this sense, Calvinism was much more of an international movement with pan-European cultural significance than was Lutheranism, which primarily affected Germanic peoples. The parish system of schooling, with a primary course at the base (although Calvin himself was little concerned with it, desirous only that children learn to read the French Bible), and a college organized to educate religious humanists and teachers devoted to reform and a pious life—this system under joint civil-ecclesiastical control became a cardinal element in the emerging representative government which characterized middle

---

[18] *Ibid.*, pp. 70–71.
[19] *Ibid.*, p. 17; F. Eby, *op. cit.*, p. 117.

class societies during the sixteenth, seventeenth, and eighteenth centuries. Colonial America, particularly New England, experienced this system and developed it into a characteristic American institution whose features in local government can still be seen today.

English educational thought. English humanism and religious purposes in education did not differ radically from those on the Continent, but there were some points of difference. The public school movement—the founding of schools catering to laymen— began in the late fourteenth century with the creation of Winchester (1387), which was followed, in the fifteenth and sixteenth centuries by the establishment of Eton, St. Paul's, and others. The later schools were encouraged by the reform carried out by Henry VIII. Most of these schools, at least up to the time of the reform, shared the fashionable aim of preparing young men for courtly, aristocratic, or clerical careers. The religious reform rendered them more broadly useful because of the relative secularization of church and administration.

As had happened on the Continent, other educational needs supported by the new middle class required fulfillment. Apparently based on the tradition of town guild schools and inspired by the example of the public schools, the Merchant Taylor's School, sponsored by the Merchant Taylor Guild, was established in 1560. A young Oxford-trained teacher, Richard Mulcaster (1530–1611), was appointed headmaster. A sensitive thinker, Mulcaster saw that this school, drawing pupils from the middle class, could not hope to place all its graduates in high-ranking positions in state and church. He reasoned that more practical studies should be provided in addition to traditional classical ones, thus allowing students to excel in those branches that most suited them. He was influenced by the Platonic conception of education, according to which children's abilities differ significantly, and therefore they require schooling and training that respond to their individual abilities. This educational idea was, of course, akin to the popular Renaissance Platonic concept of education for state service (i.e., service in court, in royal retinues, on special missions, and so on). Mulcaster felt that the school should bring out and develop the best qualities in youth, and that these qualities should serve as criteria for assigning them places in society.

As did other Renaissance thinkers, Mulcaster became convinced that teaching must take the individual child into account, and that the mother tongue had a definite place early in the educational program. He insisted on the advantage of preceding the study of classical tongues with a sound training in English, recommending that readiness to learn rather than chronological age be used as criterion for advancement. In terms of religious culture, he saw that the ability to read English was useful, but did not actually call for universal primary education. His ardent feeling for his native culture is expressed in these words: "I love Rome, but London is better. I favor Italie, but England more. I honor the Latin, but I worship the English."[20]

As a progressive humanist, Mulcaster also favored educating the ladies of families of social distinction. For fine young women he had the greatest respect, maintaining that in ability and intelligence they deserved a liberal education, notwithstanding the traditional taboos that circumscribed their activity. Since society was demanding more of women, they should receive literary, language, and moral education appropriate to their role.

Regardless of their seeming appropriateness for the educational problems of his time, Mulcaster's ideas were not given serious attention for over two centuries. Tradition-bound society could not see the logic or naturalness of his ideas. English grammar schools, although they accepted some boys who lacked financial means, remained largely the select province of the wellborn. The upbringing of gentlemen prevailed over the education of youth to live in a steadily urbanizing, commercializing society. Although Crown and Parliament in England took some measures to insure vocational education and its protection of boys' interests (masters were to provide instruction in reading and writing), society made no significant adjustment to the educational needs of a changing culture.

In the English schools, as in other Protestant schools, learning usually meant memorizing questions and answers on the catechism, Scriptural selections, and classical literature. Although mother tongues were sometimes taught, and many Protestant reformers advocated a liberal pedagogy and a pleasant classroom atmosphere, the religious demands of the Reformation turned most schools into dens for doctrine, conducted under stern discipline.

---

[20] Richard Mulcaster, *The First Part of the Elementarie* (Oxford: Oxford University Press, 1925), p. 269. A second major work of Mulcaster on education was his *Positions,* a stimulating consideration of pedagogical theory, published in 1581.

Other educational ideas

Jesuit movement.   In cultural response to the rapid development of the Protestant cause in education, Roman Catholic leaders undertook counterreform movements to establish their church on firmer footing and to compete with the new churches. History shows that the Catholics enjoyed no small success in their efforts.

One of the outstanding examples of success was the Jesuit Order (originally *Compania,* later *Societas Iesu,* or Society of Jesus), founded by the Spanish nobleman, St. Ignatius of Loyola (1491–1556) in 1539. St. Ignatius became General of the order, with full papal approval, in 1541.

The Council of Trent, which was convened in 1545, strongly urged all orders to re-establish their moral authority and resume their educational efforts. The Ursuline Order (1535) for women, and the movement of Port Royal (also referred to as Jansenist), led by St. Cyran in the seventeenth century, are good examples of educational reform undertaken by Catholic leaders.

Under the Jesuit system, the world was divided up into provinces, in each of which the Order's activities were governed by a *Provincial.* Each province had a college, administered by a rector appointed by the General in the name of the pope. Those taking the Jesuit vow enlisted to work in educating youth. By 1556, the Order controlled thirty-six schools in Italy, Sicily, Spain, Portugal, France, Germany, and Bohemia.[21] Within a few years, Jesuit institutions had sprung up in Poland, Western Russia, and the New World.

The key principle in the educational program was discipline: obedience to authority and the building of self-discipline. The main educational instrument was the full plan of studies which governed all Jesuit schools: the *Ratio Studiorum.* The program's main purpose was to educate youth in "a way that they may be brought to a knowledge and love for our Creator and Redeemer,"[22] and no teacher of philosophy could instruct without having passed the theology course. The teachers were urged to inspire religious morality, to show unquestioned obedience to authorities, and to refer only to approved literature on every possible occasion in and out of class. The scholastic tradition of theological exegesis and disputation was

---

21 Farrell, *op. cit.,* p. 25.
22 Ulich, *op. cit.,* p. 274.

preserved in this plan of studies, although humanistic learning along Renaissance lines was diligently pursued (an aim that was at the heart of Loyola's educational intention).

The schooling was organized on two levels. The lower (*not* primary) school (*studia inferiora*) was a five- to six-year program, offering courses in grammar in three different grades, with emphasis on Latin and Greek. (The occasional criticism that Jesuit education neglected Greek is not correct insofar as provision for it in the *Ratio* is concerned.) The lower school also gave instruction in classical poetry and prose (humanities) from expurgated texts (for morality's sake), and in rhetoric, covering methods of declamation according to Cicero and the main Greek authors. The higher school (*studia superiora*) offered a seven-year program in philosophy and theology. Philosophy covered, over a three-year period, the main branches of knowledge, as handed down by scholastic tradition since Aquinas, and included logic, natural philosophy (physics, mathematics, some aspects of psychology) and moral philosophy (more psychology, metaphysics, and ethics). These studies constituted essentially a liberal arts course of university rank and were largely based on Aristotle's writings, not on more recent developments in scientific fields. The advanced subject, theology, contained essentially scholastic doctrine with moral teachings based on Scriptures and sacramental matters.[23] It required four years to complete and could only be taken by experienced teachers from the higher school.

One of the truly outstanding features of the Jesuits' program was the provision for teacher education. Men teachers were selected from lower school, given a trial period to test their patience and devotion, and returned to the higher school to complete their education. They learned thoroughly the program of studies, neatly arranged in orderly sequence and progressive steps. Four years' teaching experience preceded their ordination as priests and teachers with "tenure." Here one can see, for the first time in European educational history, a well-defined plan for developing a teaching corps.

A few other features of the Jesuit system that merit special comment are its organization, tuition costs, emulation, and reward-and-punishment system. Under each college rector stood two "prefects" (each a kind of dean), one responsible for academic affairs and

---

[23] A ready summary of the Jesuit program of studies is in Farrell, *op. cit.,* pp. 342–54. For a general history of the movement, cf. Schwickerath, *op. cit.*

the other concerned with matters of discipline. This organization enabled the school to be managed efficiently along hierarchical principles that preserved the integrity of the clerical authorities. Especially good for the success of the Jesuit schools was the work of the academic prefect, whose supervisory eye helped to develop and maintain teaching standards.

For many generations Jesuit schools resembled modern public schools in that they charged no tuition: normally, the Jesuits would not establish a college without prior assurance of adequate financial endowment to pay for building and staff. Ideally, this principle would have favored boys with native ability regardless of their social origin, but because the Jesuits were not concerned with primary education and because their difficult entrance examinations demanded a level of learning hardly accessible to any but the wellborn, the social character of their schools was essentially aristocratic.

Emulation in classroom and social living was a widespread practice in Jesuit schools for the purpose of achieving peer conformity to approved behavior. Those who excelled in achieving set goals were lauded and given prizes (material things) for their efforts. Others were encouraged to surpass the winners; and frequently classes—and even schools—were divided into competing rival groups. The appeal was not made to the individual's sense of personal progress or self-evaluation, but rather to a group or institutional norm. The possibilities for group manipulation of youth in such a system are obvious.

Closely tied to emulation was the reward-and-punishment system. Honors as well as prizes were accorded to the good students, and the lack of such rewards was at once a negative recompense, or form of punishment, for the poor student. Naturally, much in European cultural history since early Greek times supported meritorious reward as a social and psychological motivation, but its perhaps excessive use by the Jesuits brought condemnation from Catholic and Protestant educators alike. More severe forms of punishment, mainly deprivation of privileges and corporal punishment, were normally used by Jesuit teachers only as a last resort. A serious misdemeanor placed a boy in the hands of the school "Corrector" (a non-Jesuit), who decided what action to take. The final word in such cases, however, rested with the Rector, and in general the history of these schools indicates a rather mild policy in correction matters.

Their eminent successes for some two hundred years in raising up new generations of social leaders, inside and outside the Roman Catholic Church, testify to the effectiveness of the Jesuit programs in education and culture. During most of that time, the Jesuits' liberal arts schools had no equals in the breadth of learning offered. As the Jesuit Order increased in political influence and in its attempts to control the thinking of society, public suspicion and animosity grew until the Order was dissolved by the papacy under state pressures (France, in 1764; Spain, in 1767; some Italian principalities, in 1768). In 1773 Pope Clement XIV ordered its full abolition.

Educational developments in eastern Europe.   Some East European areas also felt the rise in intellectual pursuits. Although Slavic Europe was not within the mainstream of European cultural and economic growth, particularly after Constantinople's fall in 1453 and the expansion of Turkish power in Europe, it gave rise to developments of historical significance for European education.

The university movement affected cultural centers in Czechoslovakia and Poland, where in 1348 and 1364, respectively, the Universities of Prague and Cracow were founded with papal and royal sanction. Cathedral and monastic schools, as well as some parish schools, functioned at that time and increased in number during the fifteenth and sixteenth centuries. In Moscovite Russia, which was not under Roman ecclesiastical law, but, rather, had adapted Byzantine canon to its clerical needs, formal schooling came somewhat later, although monastic and court education was being carried on as early as the eleventh century. The Orthodox clergy also tutored sons of the landed nobility, and during the sixteenth century numbers of reading schools were organized for such families.[24]

---

[24] For these developments consult W. F. Reddaway, *et al.,* eds., *The Cambridge History of Poland* (Cambridge: Cambridge University Press, 1950), pp. 157, 180, 282–85; K. Kharlampovich, *Zapadnorusskiia pravoslavnie shkoly XVI i nachala XVII veka* (Kazan: Imperatorskii Universitet, 1898), pp. 5–92, 98; N. A. Konstantinov *et al.,* eds., *Istoriia pedagogiki* (Moscow: Akademiia Pedagogicheskikh Nauk, 1958), pp. 179 ff.; A.M. Varchenko, "Ukrainskaia natsional'naia shkola kontsa XVI i nachala XVII stoletiiu," *Sovetskaia pedagogika,* 6 (June, 1941), 74–88; S. F. Zbanduto, "Kievskaia Akademiia XVI–XVII vv.," *Ibid.,* 7 (July, 1946), 59–75.

As seats of royal power, both Prague and Cracow nurtured educational institutions for their elites. Humanistic secondary schools and colleges arose there, as they had in Western Europe, and after the founding of the Jesuit Order a veritable mushrooming of such institutions occurred. As in the West, these efforts aimed to counter the spread of Protestantism, which—especially in Poland—was eminently successful in founding schools and converting noble and merchant families to Calvinism and Lutheranism.

This educational movement influenced Russia directly, since large areas populated by Russian-Ukrainian Orthodox subjects were within Polish territory, and many of these people were attracted to or else felt compelled to compete with the new Polish schools. The Orthodox, laymen and clerical leaders alike, formed associations (*Bratstva,* or brotherhoods) which sponsored schools organized and conducted much along the lines of Catholic and Protestant humanistic education, but with considerable intellectual, religious, and administrative traditions incorporated from Russian and Greek practices. The Russian-Ukrainian schools adapted much of the form and methodology used in Jesuit and Protestant schools (for example, the five-year grammar and humanities course), while maintaining advanced dialectic, philosophical, and religious teachings in accordance with practices of their own clergy. The more famous among the many such schools were those at Lvov, Ostrog, and Kiev, founded in the late sixteenth and early seventeenth centuries. It was at this time that the Russians first encountered the humanistic literary works of Homer, Virgil, Ovid, Cicero, Aristotle, and as well the complete works of some Greek Church Fathers. Many of the graduates of the new brotherhood schools—particularly of the one at Kiev, developed by Bishop Peter Mohyla (Mogila) in the 1620's and 1630's—went to Moscow in order to serve in educational institutions there. Later they were also very influential in the court of Peter the Great (1689–1725), who sought to modernize Russian education.

CHAPTER IV

Emergence of Modern Educational Ideas in the Seventeenth and Eighteenth Centuries

Education for Modern Man

Nothing should be learned solely for its value at school, but for its use in life.

Comenius

There is truly no break between the preceding period of Renaissance and Reformation and the seventeenth and eighteenth centuries. Most of the ideas in education and learning that will be discussed here had already appeared, in one form or another, during that exciting period of human development and creativity. But the modernity of those ideas began to take on more concrete form and the ideas themselves began actually to assume the character of movements—not everywhere in Europe or America, but certainly in many countries and in many ways. The unfolding of scientific knowledge and thought, at the same time that the reforms were being established, created a new kind of tension in Western traditions, not unlike that felt by the Greeks when the Ionian philosophers began asking all those disturbing questions. Could religion and science really both teach?

There was one man who belonged in both camps, whose convictions were religious but whose attitudes towards educational problems showed that he understood and accepted much that the "new" sciences were producing in knowledge. This man was Jan Amos Komensky (Comenius), a Moravian bishop whose thinking was at least two hundred years ahead of his time (1592–1670). To judge from his educational and religious writings, Comenius was not conscious of any conflicts between religion and science. In a way he stood between the rebels (such as Rabelais) and the scholastics (such as Loyola, and perhaps Calvin on the Protestant side), taking a position that found common ground between supernaturalism and naturalism. Although his ideas were not original or revolutionary, his applications of these ideas presented great new possibilities for educational leaders. It is in this sense that Comenius may be considered a propagator of modern ideas.

Education according to Comenius.   Born of modest Protestant (Moravian Brothers) parents in Moravia, Jan Comenius managed to acquire an elementary, grammar, and university education, including three years in Germany. He became both pastor and teacher, but the Thirty Years' War (1618–48) forced him to spend most of his life abroad—in Poland, Hungary, Sweden, England, and Holland. Everywhere he taught, studied, and wrote on pedagogical subjects. Through his early association with Wolfgang Ratke (1571–1635) in Germany, Comenius received ideas on sense realism and scientific methods popularized by Francis Bacon and adherents of the new knowledge.[1] Comenius pursued these interests, and through his humble background, his sufferings, his keen feelings for his subjugated homeland, and his experience with the horrors of war, he became deeply conscious of the need for a completely new education—not only for his own people, but also for the whole of mankind in the Christian world. In the hopes of laying the groundwork for such an education, he published some revolutionary educational materials and put out grandiose schemes for uniting men's minds and hearts.

Quoting Diogenes (413–327 B.C.), Comenius asked, "What is the foundation of every state? The education of its youth." Comenius believed that education should have a broad social base and consist of early home training under the mother's care, followed by a six-year primary school in which the native tongue would be the language of instruction. This plan, like that of other religious reformers, was intended to provide a common cultural experience for all children and to substitute a sense of national solidarity for the keen class consciousness reinforced by intellectual studies in foreign languages (Greek and Latin) at an early age. Comenius would have able pupils advance into the secondary (Latin grammar)

---

[1] On Comenius, cf. M. W. Keatinge, *The Great Didactic of John Amos Comenius* (London: Adam and Charles Black, Ltd., 1896); Vladimir Jelinek, ed. and trans., *Comenius: Analytical Didactic* (Chicago: University of Chicago Press, 1953); A. A. Krasnovskii, ed., *Ian Amos Komenskii. Izbrannye pedagogicheskikh sochinenii* (Moscow: Uchpedgiz, 1955); UNESCO, *John Amos Comenius, 1592–1670,* with an Introduction by Jean Piaget (Paris: UNESCO, 1957).

school for another six-year program. Capable graduates of this school went on to the university for professional studies. The entire scheme embodied, in theory, a socially nondiscriminating principle (except for its religious purpose). The universal and—to a considerable extent—revolutionary concept of education that Comenius endorsed was most explicit in the very title of his most important work, *The Great Didactic,* which in its entirety continues as follows: "Setting forth The Whole Art of Teaching all Things to All Men, or A certain Inducement to found such Schools in all the Parishes, Towns, and Villages of every Christian Kingdom, that the entire Youth of both Sexes, None being excepted, shall, Quickly, Pleasantly, Thoroughly Become learned in the Sciences, pure in Morals, Trained in Piety, and in this manner Instructed in all things necessary for the present and for the future life."[2] A more inclusive —and, no doubt, impossible for the time—educational program could not be found in the seventeenth century.

Children's active human senses, Comenius insisted, should be used in learning. He encouraged pupils to observe and work with natural objects, to examine live things and study their characteristics. Pupils should ask about and discuss real information as well as write it down when it has been learned. To encourage use of this more active method, Comenius published the first illustrated "visual aid" textbook for the study of Latin language and the sciences: *Orbis Pictus (The World in Pictures),* in 1658. Organized in series of topics (e.g., God, world, air, water, earth, metals, flowers, vegetables, and so on), the book has an illustration of each object and, in short sentences, tells something about it.[3]

After primary school, in which use of the mother tongue enlivened the child's notions of the world about him, Comenius would have pupils study "real" and practical subjects: natural sciences, geography, medicine, the mechanical arts, and history (including notions about the history of various disciplines or subjects).

As a basic teaching method for children, Comenius advocated going from the general to the particular, from the easy to the more difficult, from the near to the distant. Although a logical sequence

---

[2] F. Eby, *The Development of Modern Education,* 2nd ed. (Englewood Cliffs, N.J.: Prentice-Hall, Inc., 1952), p. 200.

[3] A good example of the method is in the following edition of his "visible world" volume: *Orbis sensualium pictus* (London: S. Leacroft, 1777).

should be followed within a subject, teachers should connect each subject with others and not insist on a memorization of isolated subject matter. These principles were elaborated in detail in his *Magna Didactica*.

Comenius related all his ideas to religion by reasoning that since the main goal of education is to bring individuals to glorify God, the most effective ways for understanding His creation should be found through schooling. All children of all countries can profit from such an educational experience, he felt, and this universal appeal for national systems of education was an early call for a mass cultural effort by the civilized world, predating mass popular systems of education in nation-states by nearly three hundred years. God's beneficence and mercy, he felt, were plain in the great opportunity mankind had to educate all children intelligently. Mass primary education and learning through firsthand experience of the knowledge to be acquired had social and moral values as well as did religious instruction. Essential virtues, he thought, included wisdom, moderation, artistic skills, truthfulness, courage, and diligence.

Even though Comenius's proposals came at a time when, especially in northern Europe, a commercial revolution was producing more wealth and an ambitious middle class amenable to a new, practical education for its children, and although a narrow religious humanism seemed already to be obsolete, his ideas did not seem to find rapid assimilation. To be sure, his texts were read and often used in schools; they were rendered in many languages, and even in Moscow during the early years of Peter the Great's reign the *Orbis Pictus* found use in the secondary school.[4] But Jan Comenius did not enjoy the confidence of those authorities who could impose the kinds of sociocultural changes that his educational ideas called for.

Science and Education

> The business of education . . . is not . . . to make them perfect in any one of the sciences, . . . but to open and dispose their minds. . . .
>
> *Locke*

Scientific knowledge and learning. If the Moravian bishop could not break down the wall between religion and science, what was the fate of science in the schools, and what other apparent

---

[4] Alexander Lipski, "The Beginning of General Secondary Education in Russia," *History of Education Journal*, VI, 3 (Spring, 1955), 204–205.

effects did it have on educational thought? The thread of scientific thought.had slowly but surely gained in strength and tenacity since the late medieval period, when Roger Bacon postulated that observation and experimental methods, involving the proof of things, were the true and scientific foundation of knowledge. Social criticism, sense realism, and rationalism all helped to reintroduce, during the sixteenth and seventeenth centuries, the spirit of inquiry that brought about revolutions in knowledge. The breakup of the universal church, although it did not lead immediately to complete liberty and acceptance of scientific thinking on the part of the churches (Luther and Calvin both held to traditional astronomy), ended the monopoly on the teaching of knowledge held by one clerical hierarchy. This fact, together with the growing social importance of the commercial classes who challenged the old cosmology and explanations of cause, produced a climate in which new learnings could find the light of day.

For several centuries during the Renaissance, what was "new" was actually "old," and classical achievements in scientific thought were usually the only ones accepted by the schools. The geographic explorations were the chief exception to this state of affairs until well into the sixteenth century. Gradually criticism undermined teachings about the universe, the elements, and animal life. The Christian doctrine of God as creator and spiritual intercessor to redeem humans assisted in building this new attitude by opposing ancient beliefs in a mixed supernaturalistic and naturalistic world, wherein spirits and matter-forms were coincident and gods took human forms. Christianity helped partition this mixture, leaving concern for the natural world to human thought. The step from there to reason, observation, and experiment was a short one. All three had in fact been voiced by the fourteenth century, but conditions for their exercise had not developed. During the sixteenth and sventeenth centuries, these methods largely dismantled classical science and began to build a new one, based on the primacy of matter and material organization. Acceptance of this science has extended down into the twentieth century, when new physics and intellectual thought are raising questions about the validity of this order.[5]

There was, however, no place in the traditional school for the

---

[5] See a nice discussion of science and intellectual positions in Werner Heisenberg, *Physics and Philosophy* (New York: Harper & Row, Publishers, 1958).

new science. Still oriented predominantly toward medieval logic, religious morality, and church aims, the school could not accommodate the new science. It therefore "caused no sudden break in the course of academic studies, nor did it suddenly enable a 'scientific method' of investigation to prove its value."[6] To some extent, medical teachings—enriched by full recourse to original sources and by a few New World drugs—altered their medieval curriculum. The publication of scientific works up to 1500 shows this general sterility, in terms of new knowledge, of Renaissance science (cf. A. C. Klebs, "Incunabula Scientifica et Medica," in *Orbis,* Vol. IV, 1938).[7]

Beginning in Italy, and influencing progressively the rest of Europe, scientific inquiry produced a series of great scientific and technical innovations that changed the very content of man's knowledge about his physical world. The following are outstanding representatives in the indicated fields:

> da Vinci (1452–1519): comparative anatomy, mechanics
> Copernicus (1473–1543): astronomy, heliocentrism
> Vesalius (1514–1564): human anatomy
> Galileo (1564–1642): telescopic magnifying lens, heliocentric theory
> Kepler (1571–1630): planetary movements
> Descartes (1596–1650): analytical geometry
> von Guericke (1602–1686): air pump; electrical machine
> Torricelli (1608–1647): barometer
> Pascal (1623–1662): calculating machine, laws of atmospheric pressure
> Boyle (1627–1691): chemistry, law of gases
> Newton (1643–1727): gravitation, laws of motion, calculus
> Leibniz (1646–1716): calculus

It should be added that all these men profited from earlier workers in these fields and from the total scientific heritage; they were able to put to better use algebra, geometry, and methods of reasoning developed centuries before.

Where did these new sciences find "refuge"? Where could men cultivate and teach them? Who supported the efforts of these men? The answers to these questions are still far from complete. Some support did come from the new class—the merchants and well-to-do

---

[6] A. R. Hall, *The Scientific Revolution, 1500–1800* (London: Longmans, Green & Company, Ltd., 1954), p. 69. The present writer is much indebted to Mr. Hall's discussion of this fascinating period of intellectual and scientific history.

[7] See Appendix C, in *ibid.,* pp. 371 ff.

townspeople, such as Thomas Gresham of London and the de' Medici family in Florence. Royal courts, anxious to acquire more power and influence, sometimes aided scientific and technical efforts. In Elizabethan England in the 1560's, members of the royal Government were already entertaining ideas about establishing schools with a modern, practical curriculum, so that young noblemen would be, as one adviser put it, "good for some what, whereas now the most part of them are good for nothing."[8] But formal institutions did not immediately open their doors to the new disciplines, and for a long time correspondence, friendships, and informal gatherings were the loci of discussion and exploration. Gradually, royal charters were granted to groups of eminent thinkers; new academic societies were sometimes formed on governmental initiative. Sir Francis Bacon (1561–1626), in his *New Atlantis,* described a model organization for scientific pursuits that was to influence later founders. Comenius advanced a similar idea for a scientific college.

In Italy, the academy concept was most popular, and from 1500 to 1800 some 2200 special academies were established. Fortunately, they did not all survive. The earliest seems to have been the Academia Secretorum Naturae, founded at Naples in 1560. In 1603, the Accademia dei Lincei was established (and was soon joined by Galileo). The more famous Accademia del Cimento, established in Florence in 1657, was shortlived but dedicated to experimental work. In 1662 a group of thinkers who had been meeting informally for over fifteen years received a royal charter and became the Royal Society of London for the promotion of Natural Knowledge. (Unfortunately, Crown and Parliament failed to grant an endowment.) In France, Colbert established the Académie des Sciences in 1666, but French thinkers (Descartes, Pascal, Mersenne, Fermat, and others) had been holding meetings and discussions for some thirty years, and literary academies had been established before the scientific Académie. The German Academia Naturae Curiosi, founded in Leipzig in 1652, published annual accounts of scientific activities long before the more official Berlin Societas Regia Scientarium (later the Deutsche Akadamie der Wissenschaften) was founded in 1700. In Russia, Peter the Great's wife, Catherine I, fulfilled his plan for an Imperial Akademiia Nauk in January, 1725. In the

---

[8] See account in W. H. G. Armytage, *Four Hundred Years of English Education* (Cambridge: Cambridge University Press, 1963), Chap. 1.

Anglo-American colonies, Benjamin Franklin's initiative led to creation of the American Philosophical Society in 1743.

Many other academies and societies were organized in the European world during this two-hundred-year period, but few inroads were made by science into established educational institutions. Some new courses of mathematics and natural sciences appeared at Cambridge University. Most progress made, however, came through the establishment of new schools. A successful venture was launched in Germany by August Francke (1663–1727), who established secondary schools in which modern science subjects—including laboratory techniques in chemistry and physics—were taught together with humanistic and religious studies.[9] In 1747, one of his students, Julius Hecker (1707–68), founded a scientific school (Realschule) for boys seeking a practical rather than humanistic education. The program stressed mathematics and natural sciences, and included many activities through which the students acquired knowledge by doing experiments, work, and visitations related to their subjects. In certain ways, this program followed the thinking and suggestions of the "realists"—Montaigne, Rabelais, Vives, Comenius, and (to some extent) Mulcaster.

The new educational tendency, sponsored by German Pietist reformers, became popular in the eighteenth century and led to the establishment of a good number of scientific secondary schools in German lands. This type of school had its counterpart in few other countries, but a mathematics school was established in England before 1700, and in Russia Tsar Peter established the Mathematics and Navigation School in 1701—the first such school entirely devoted to a program of mathematics and science. The nonconformist "dissenting academies" in England presented (from about midseventeenth century) a modern curriculum formulated along lines suggested by John Milton. It offered instruction in mathematics, natural sciences, geography, anatomy, astronomy, navigation, and other practical and civic subjects. At about the same time, similar studies appeared in some French academies established under royal and noble patronage. A century later, North America saw the rise of the academy movement, with practical and modern studies.[10]

---

9 Eby, *op. cit.*, p. 253.

10 On scientific, utilitarian, and modern civic studies, see I. L. Kandel, *History of Secondary Education* (Boston: Houghton Mifflin Company, 1930), pp. 150 ff.; Eby, *op. cit.*, pp. 253–64.

The whole scientific movement, linked as it was (if unwittingly) to the changing social patterns and cultural needs of European and American societies, had by the eighteenth century begun to pene-trate the crust of traditional humanistic education that had gradually succeeded scholastic studies. It did so painfully and not without giving rise to violent outbursts of human wrath and ignorance: the Catholic Inquisition, and the horrible witch hunts and trials perpetrated by both Protestant and Catholic communities,[11] were among the blackest and most inhuman cultural perversions in Western history—occurring on the very doorstep of the Enlightenment and the Modern Age. Yet, one of the greatest intellects leading the scientific advance, Sir Isaac Newton, paid tribute to Divinity:

> This most beautiful system of the sun, planets, and comets, can only proceed from the counsel and dominion of an intelligent and powerful Being. . . . He endures forever, and is everywhere present; and by existing always and everywhere, he constitutes duration and space.[12]

Others paid similar tribute. But the traditionalists and dogmatists had no argument with these professions of faith or even with the activities of these men; rather, it was with the new knowledge that undermined the intellectual foundations of their archaic social system and positions of human power that the church leaders felt obliged to fight. Secular authority saw such advantages in the new science, however, that its advance seemed assured, if occasionally harassed. Yet the great universities viewed these practical disciplines as vulgar pursuits. The new University of Halle (1694), and later that at Göttingen (1734), were exceptions.

The new ideas in education and the new knowledge received little or no support from the privileged classes, the aristocracy and the clergy. The merchant class—the "new class"—gave what support it could within the restrictive laws and customs controlling education in the various countries; and royalty, usually for reasons of finance or power, sometimes worked to break down old barriers of feudal aristocracy blocking commerce and the growth of useful knowledge.

[11] On the witch fanaticism, see the account in Edgar N. Johnson, *An Introduction to the History of the Western Tradition,* Vol. II (Boston: Ginn & Company, 1959), pp. 143–45, 156–58.

[12] A. R. Hall, *The Scientific Revolution, 1500–1800* (London: Longmans, Green & Company, Ltd., 1954), p. 271. Reprinted by permission of Longmans, Green & Co.

Documentation of these sources of support is beyond the purpose of this survey, but it is a task that needs to be seriously undertaken.[13]

Attention must now be focussed on a few of the great architects of new educational theory who wrote a cultural response to the explosion of knowledge, much in the same way that the Greeks had responded to the Ionian philosophers of science. Comenius, already discussed, was a precursor to the thinkers of the latter seventeenth and eighteenth centuries. These men departed significantly from the rationalistic, formal discipline concept championed by the less experimental thinkers who followed Cartesian thought and were heirs of scholastic tradition, although some (e.g., John Locke) retained notions attributable to the formal position.[14]

John Locke (1632–1704). Locke was not the innovator or revolutionary thinker in educational affairs that he sometimes is made out to have been. But he certainly provided an historical and worthy service by synthesizing many of the ideas that had accumulated for nearly two hundred years—ideas that dissented from the classical literary and religion-bound humanism. He presented these ideas in a context that fitted neatly into the growing body of political thought championing the equality of human beings in terms of their civil liberties. He himself contributed much to the propagation of these political ideas. Locke postulated, fundamentally, that men are substantially equal in their biological makeup; a moral corollary to that idea was that men should enjoy equal opportunity to govern themselves.[15] Finally, Locke emphasized a psychology that rejected traditional views of the human mind as divided into separate faculties. His own education at Oxford retraced in most respects those practices that had been built up since the twelfth century—with heavy doses of rhetorical and logical exercises, disputations and declamations—that religious and academic authorities had come to prize as education. Locke cultivated a peculiar distaste for this type of education. Born into a Puritan family of moderate means, but later converted to Anglicanism, Locke early showed an interest in

---

13 See Armytage, *op. cit.*

14 A brief statement on formal discipline is in Elmer H. Wilds and K. V. Lottich, *The Foundations of Modern Education,* 3rd ed. (New York: Holt, Rinehart & Winston, Inc., 1961), pp. 228 ff.

15 See Locke's *Of Civil Government* (London: J. M. Dent & Sons, Ltd. 1943), especially Book II, Chaps. 2, 8. For example, "Men being ... by nature all free, equal, and independent, no one can be ... subjected to the political power of another without his own consent . . ." (p. 164).

physical causes and phenomena, especially in experiments in chemistry and medicine. This interest left a mark upon his philosophical views concerning knowledge, which he defined as based on sense perceptions that are then subject to inner reflection. This viewpoint largely determined both his theory of learning and his educational philosophy. During stays in Holland and France, Locke extended his knowledge and shared his ideas with other thinkers.

His two main works dealing with educational ideas were *Some Thoughts concerning Education* and *An Essay Concerning the Understanding, Knowledge, Opinion, and Assent.* He perceived an important sociological fact: that custom is stronger than natural law, binding people to idolize common practices that perpetuate backwardness and ignorance. He would have this stumbling block to educational progress removed and those with merit educated as far as their capacities allow. No time should be wasted, however, with dull students.

What was novel in his theories was his conception of the mind as having an open-ended, undetermined intelligence. He held no a priori claims on the human mind, maintaining that it behaves according to the impressions cultural stimuli make upon it. The human mind was for him a tabula rasa—a clean slate. He recognized no innate laws governing thought, intelligence, or morality—these, he believed, are acquired in the culture as man receives impressions and directs his thinking to those things that are most necessary to him. He did admit that men differ in their characters. He opposed long-held beliefs about the virtue of exercising the memory, the theory of transfer of training (e.g., a knowledge of Latin grammar is helpful to learning mathematics), and the beneficial effects of heavy educational burdens for young children. On the last question, Locke favored a growth theory that demanded of children only that of which they were capable. This attitude did not countenance "softness"; on the contrary, he roundly mocked those who pampered children: "For if the Child must have Grapes or Sugar-plums, when he has a Mind to them, rather than make the poor Baby cry . . . ," then when he is grown up he will lack character and be led astray.[16]

Locke would have youngsters exposed to weather and not overly protected from the elements. Water in his shoes does not harm young

---

[16] John Locke, *Some Thoughts Concerning Education,* with Introduction and Notes by Rev. R. H. Quick (Cambridge: Cambridge University Press, 1902), p. 22.

Jack but, rather, conditions his body to resist the elements. Nor would Locke neglect drill and habit formation, which form the basis of mastery in learning. Recognizing that society in his day required many kinds of skills on the part of adults, Locke advocated various kinds and levels of education: modern languages, classical languages and literature, preparation for business, and so on. To learn to use a modern language, Locke believed, the best method is the direct one—speaking instead of laboring over grammar. Locke would have a "modern" curriculum designed to produce a liberally educated young man: English, foreign languages, mathematics, drawing, geography, history, ethics, law, and natural science.

Notwithstanding his many progressive ideas, Locke did not depart substantially from tradition on a number of questions. He did not oppose social segregation or its hold on education. His preference for the tutorial method over class instruction for the elite was consistent with the concept of aristocratic privilege. He did suggest that society assume some responsibility for popular education, but this idea was hardly new. Like most good humanists, he held religious virtue in high esteem as a main foundation for youth education.

Locke's greatest importance lay in his rejection of rationalism-idealism—i.e., a metaphysical system—as the main intellectual method of knowing and learning. He did not trust logic and so felt more secure in an empirical, sense-realist position. This established him as the first modern psychologist in educational theory.[17] His influential writings helped bring on and stimulate the century of Enlightenment, rich in new educational speculations, plans, and works. Locke was perhaps the last of the truly great, creative educational thinkers in England, and many of his concepts remained modern into the nineteenth century, serving as guidelines for a changing social order that witnessed the rise of the middle class to power and influence.

Les philosophes and Rousseau.   To close this chapter with a focus on the French thinkers on human progress and the most important social critic of the century, Rousseau, is to ignore a host of other great thinkers and the continuously changing educational scene in much of Europe. To leave out Leibniz, Kant, Hume, Berkeley, Novikov, and their concern for learning is a sore sacrifice. But the eighteenth century—a period of great intellectual, scientific,

---

17 Cf. F. Mueller, *Histoire de la psychologie* (Paris: Payot, 1960), pp. 233 ff.

economic, and political change—presents so many names that a full discussion of each is quite beyond our scope here. (Some remarks on actual educational changes will indeed follow in Chapter V.)

An analysis of the speculative ideas and schemes of these French thinkers is most useful because they produced such a tremendous store of literature on all the fundamental questions of the human condition and its relationship to man's upbringing and education. They were also representative of the new social force of the age: they were nearly all men of middle class—bourgeois—background, as were the creative thinkers in England.[18] The *philosophies* envisioned man as master of his environment—through which mastery he could embark on the road to unending progress. These views were the sharpest departure from scholastic and classical humanist traditions that the postmedieval world had witnessed. The educational plans that emerged from their intellectual cauldron were blueprints for the twentieth century.

The men of the enlightenment cast their doubts, inquiries, curiosity, and experiments onto every area of human concern. Accepting most of what had come from the natural scientists, and especially from Locke and Newton, they used the new cosmology to tear down the old with its scholastic, dualistic, and hierarchical practices.

One of the earliest propagators of the new faith of material science was Julien de La Mettrie (1709–51), who first adhered to the Port Royal movement but later rejected religious beliefs altogether. In his *Traité de l'ame* (1745), he described perception as a product of sensation alone, the senses being connected to a general nervous system. Living matter began in elementary form in slime. There can be no separation of matter from ideas—a concept he accepted from Epicurus.[19] At the same time, sense realism and the growing

---

[18] Roland Mousnier and Ernest Labrousse, *Le XVIII⁵ siècle: révolution intellectuelle, technique et politique (1715–1815)* (Paris: Presses universitaires de France, 1953), p. 75. For additional background of French thought in the Enlightenment, see also Mousnier's *Progrès scientifique et technique au XVIII⁵ siècle* (Paris: Librairie Plon, 1958), especially Introduction and Chap. 1. In English, see Hall, *op. cit.*; and Abraham Wolf, *A History of Science, Technology, and Philosophy in the 18th Century*, 2nd ed., rev. by D. McKie (London: Allen & Unwin, 1952). Crane Brinton's *The Shaping of the Modern Mind* (1958) gives a nice summary of the period. The *philosophies'* views are well portrayed in Carl L. Becker, *The Heavenly City of the Eighteenth Century Philosophers,* 11th ed. (New Haven: Yale University Press, 1955).

[19] Cf. Mueller, *op. cit.,* p. 262 ff. On the eighteenth century materialists' philosophy, cf. also G. Plekhanov (N. Bel'tov), *The Development of the Monist View of History* (Moscow: Foreign Languages Publishing House, 1956), pp. 14–25.

importance of material exploitation and production in human economy led in a similar direction. Control over matter came through the senses feeding impressions to the brain. By this mechanistic view of human behavior, La Mettrie sought to develop a new psychology that could examine the human condition rather than condemn it from rigid moral standpoints that required burial alive as punishment for some antisocial acts. He anticipated much that the other materialists advanced during the remainder of the eighteenth century.

Other materialists-atheists expanded on materialist concepts in all directions. Diderot (1713–84) worked in the fields of art, literature, and educational matters, and he directed the compilation of the great *Encyclopédie* (1751 ff.), which replaced Aquinas's *Summa Theologiae* as the intellectual standard of the scientific age. The 130 compilers of the work came mostly from the middle class and were imbued with utilitarian, practical, and rationalistic values. The royal French Council's order of March 8, 1759, followed by that of the Vatican on September 3rd, to cease publication of the encyclopedia halted this revolutionary effort to spread knowledge but failed to halt the circulation of ideas. Diderot himself, who advised Empress Catherine II of Russia on establishing national education, wrote that "From the prime minister to the lowest peasant, it is good for every one to know how to read, write, and count." A curriculum of "reading, writing, arithmetic, and religion" should be offered to all children.[20]

Others, like Helvetius (1715–71), Holbach (1723–89), Buffon (1707–88), and Cabanis (1757–1808)—to name a few—all elaborated in their own way a material conception of life. Since everything real was susceptible to sense perception, man's only obstacle is ignorance and the social and moral customs that prevent him from obtaining knowledge and using it to make him materially satisfied, happy. The logical line of action then is to master the environment, to perfect it so that its material conditions—which are the only reality—will render life perfect. An unending line of progress was seen as the inevitable result of such mastery. Since all was matter, the use of scientific method and reason must be taught so as to overcome all false custom and habits of ignorance. Culture

20 Gabriel Compayre, *The History of Pedagogy*, W. H. Payne, trans. (Boston: D. C. Heath & Company, 1901), pp. 320–21.

and education thus become entirely things of human need and interest, which create moral and social forms in the culture. Education must then be functional, not doctrinal. This view broke absolutely and finally with the sacred traditions that held the primary purposes in education to be religious.

That environment was everything was a postulate that the materialist thinkers never actually set out to prove; rather, they deduced it from available scientific data and so, in one way, belied their basic belief in the omniscient nature of sense experience. Had they abandoned their own adherence to the beliefs that common opinion and the power of custom are the forces governing society, they might have advanced to the point of the Marxists, holding to a scientific materialism and economic determinism.

Except for Diderot and Helvetius, the materialists' educational views were little developed. They held that education is capable of completely determining the individual's makeup. In principle, they all held that the manipulation of man's environment was the way to social and moral progress. A clear elaboration of the revolutionary, public education programs that corresponded to the materialists' ideas had to await the First Republic, when both theoretical and actual developments in French education flourished. (These will be discussed in Chapter V.)

Coincident with the materialist philosophy in France was the thinking of that great moralizer and social theorist, Jean-Jacques Rousseau (1712–78), son of a humble Genevese family. Holding firmly to a belief in the essential integrity and goodness of the individual, to the conscious training of the will, and to the need for human liberty, Rousseau departed fundamentally from the view of the materialists, although he too stood for radical reform. He did not make material necessity the father of the supreme human qualities; rather, he stated that conscience is the expression of soul. This moralistic, almost metaphysical, outlook was combined with an intense passion for life and mankind. Lapsing into indulgent sentimentalism, Rousseau sometimes led himself into sad circumstances —depravity, poverty, despair. But he would liberate man from society's cruel customs to construct a better government.

Rousseau wrote two major works, based mainly on his readings, reflections, and experiences (which did not include teaching of any consequence). These were: *Emile,* a treatise on natural education, including a brief section on girls' upbringing; and *Julie, ou la nouvelle Héloïse,* which deals at length with children's nature. In terms of pedagogical depth and interpretation, *Emile* is the more powerful of the two and, in its time (published in 1762, a year after *Héloïse*), the clearest call to educational reform.

To free man from the vices of society, Rousseau believed, it is necessary to educate him outside of society, in nature. This position establishes Rousseau as a naturalist, but not a materialist. He saw nature's (the divine) laws endowing man and the world with potential good, waiting for man to learn them in the most practical way and gradually to gain more mastery over his environment. Emile, for instance, learns the codes of morality and civic life by which he agrees to live (preparation, in a way, for the theory of the social contract). In this manner the child gradually builds up an individual culture, including spiritual values, which make him an intelligent, useful, and sensitive member of society.

His emphasis on both human nature and the external natural world enabled Rousseau to construct a pedagogy that considered the growth and interests of the child in relation to his environment. Sense experience thus became primordial in the learning process, excluding adult-imposed standards on education. The social corollary to this position was to close the door on society, on the "unnatural" world, so that its nefarious influences could not interfere with the good and natural upbringing of the child. Popularly called the "negative" approach to education, it implies a kind of censorship on the intellectual experience of children. Otherwise, the goal was full freedom to experiment with nature's wonders.

Rousseau's program for Emile has been nicely summarized in *Emile for Today.*[21] Only the outlines of the program can be suggested here. In infancy, Emile learns to talk and walk and to imitate the other skills needed to move around in his immediate environment. He learns to respond only to things, not to others' wills. Until he reaches the age of twelve, his education in the natural world continues. He acquires basic notions of science—such as heat, cold, hardness, softness, height, depth—as the direct result of the contact of his senses with the immediate environment, and as a function of his freely moving about. In contrast, his movements in "civilized"

---

21 William Boyd, *Emile for Today.* (London: William Heinemann, Limited, 1958). Used by permission of the publisher, Heinemann, Educational Books Ltd.

society are subjected to a multitude of rules or regimes imposed by adults. On these points the materialist philosophers made common cause with Rousseau.

On the other hand, Rousseau discounted the rational ability of children. He rather encouraged the tutorial system—and this is the only form of education he envisoned—to impose restrictions on childlike inquisitiveness by giving irrational answers until the youth reached what Rousseau considered to be the rational age. This negative method he chose to term *regulated liberty*. It was his way of leading the child to understand the rational world, which held only good in store for him. This understanding was, he thought, of supreme importance to the average child, not the exceptional one. Notwithstanding his tutorship formula, Rousseau saw his pedagogy as fit for making good citizens.

Boyhood requires not verbal, but *actual* learning, and this comes about only through personal experience with things that bear "on their present and obvious interest."[22] Rousseau rejects drilling children in the "basic" subjects: language, history, geography, arithmetic, and reading. Emile should approach subject matter only when his reasoning powers are adequate and knowledge becomes meaningful. Until the age of twelve, he should receive vigorous physical training and sense training—thus a foundation is laid for subsequent education.

In adolescence, Emile's mental and physical powers begin to mature; he readies himself for the more orderly intellectual and physical activities which nature demands of him and which can be made useful: practical studies with a scientific orientation, manual labor, and planned excursions into nature.[23] One discovery leads logically to another. Nature provides her own instructional materials:

> One fine evening we go for a walk in a suitable place where the open horizon allows a full view of the setting sun, and we note by landmarks the place of its setting. Next day, . . . we come back . . . to the same spot. . . . During the night the verdure has acquired a new vigour. The dawning day with its first golden beams reveals it

---

[22] *Ibid.*, p. 47.

[23] Such experiences enable Emile to master a number of useful skills that in daily life earn a living for those who practice them. In this sense Emile gradually prepares himself "for life." This idea responded well to the utilitarian interests of the merchant class.

covered with a glittering network of dew. The birds join in chorus to salute the Father of life.[24]

Emile experiences such real lessons until he is sixteen, when more systematic learning begins to take place, since he can now judge and reason. Mastery of language and literature now makes sense, and Emile's character takes definite shape. The relation of his own experience as an individual to that of others is now truly educative, and subject matter assists this process. Social education is the goal, but Emile cannot yet be exposed to all the urban ways; he must first understand proper, honorable, and healthy social relationships, and learn compassion for those human beings deprived of them.

After he reaches the age of eighteen, the "age of humanity," Emile's social education increases with historical studies, especially good biographies so as to eliminate as much distortion as possible. Moral education through fables—but without the inclusion of the pointed moral at the end—can now be useful. Such fables will help Emile to adopt the proper conduct, and not the artificiality that pervades the society around him. Religious questions should now be discussed so as to familiarize the boy with notions about the Divine Being, but without imposing a specific doctrinal belief. Later Emile will choose the religious faith that best meets his needs and interest, rather than have to follow a creed passed on to him by his parents. In any case Emile should not be exposed to the idolatrous, anthropomorphic concepts of God that are normally foisted on children.

By the time he is twenty, Emile is ready to learn all the facts of life. With this knowledge, he can guide himself through knowledge and not be protected by ignorance, since in manhood he faces many trials and the responsibility of marriage. Emile plunges into reading good books and practicing eloquent speech. Latin becomes his second language, and he must master its grammar and prose. Drama and poetry provide him with a sense of beauty and pleasure, which come more fully when he reads them in the original (thus other languages—Greek, Italian—are needed). These studies polish the young man, making him a true gentleman and the capable head of a household.

Although Rousseau's theory of education could hardly thrive under conditions of modern society—even in his time—because of

---

[24] Boyd, *op. cit.*, p. 73.

the myriad influences to which youngsters are exposed, it presents an extremely sensible guide to pedagogical principles that promote each child's learning abilities without exposing him to externally imposed values and requirements. Rousseau's children are free natural agents: free to experience and free from social customs. His theory enunciated several major ideas that, although not entirely new in historical thought, influenced the greatest nineteenth century reformers: educability is linked to growth; learning comes by doing; morals are relative to need, time, and place; and real learning must be individualized and, therefore, subjective.

In other writings, Rousseau described education as necessary for good citizenship and as a foundation for nationalism. It was impossible, he thought, to maintain a national state without public education, which naturally falls under government jurisdiction. He anticipated here those who, in the later eighteenth century, advanced ambitious plans for universal public education. (Some of these plans, as well as certain influences of Rousseau and the *philosophies* on other societies and thinkers, are discussed in Chapter V.)

A final note of "Enlightenment" pedagogy echoed, in a more practical way than through the grandiose schemes of the *philosophies,* in the experiments in sense-realist education of Johann Pestalozzi (1746–1827), a pioneer Swiss reformer. Following the call of Rousseau for a return to natural methods, Pestalozzi elaborated ideas on object lessons and on teaching in accordance with children's growth. His more celebrated writings include *Leonard and Gertrude* (1781) and *How Gertrude Teaches Her Children* (1801). Pestalozzi argued that it was education's major task to lead the child naturally along the path that its physical and intellectual development, and also its social environment, marked out for it. For good teaching to achieve this goal in method, he insisted on a tender, mutually respectful relationship between pupil and teacher rather than one of authoritarian, adult imposition.[25] The best methods, he believed, were those dependent upon nature itself and upon the active participation of children in activities related to the subject matter being studied.

---

[25] Cf. John S. Brubacher, *A History of the Problems of Education* (New York: McGraw-Hill Book Company, 1947), pp. 212–15; W. Boyd, *The History of Western Education* (London: Adam and Charles Black, Ltd., 1921), pp. 337 ff.; Robert R. Rusk, *The Doctrines of the Great Educators* (London: Macmillan & Co., Ltd., 1954), Chap. IX.

Instruction and classes divorced from life's realities were unthinkable to Pestalozzi. Arithmetic instruction was based upon counting steps, the rotations of a wheel, or the strands of thread being spun. Geography lessons included a walk to a nearby valley running north and south, or east and west. The kindly, but often inept, Swiss reformer thus introduced real objects—those that Comenius and Rousseau tried to popularize—into the lesson. The importance of understanding children and their own values was another important aspect of this unusual man's educational credo. He believed in the goodness of human nature and felt optimistic about the possibilities of improving society.

CHAPTER V

National Systems of Education:
Some Leading Ideas and Types of Systems

> If the indefinite improvement of our species is . . . a general law
> of nature, man ought no longer to regard himself as . . . limited
> to a transitory and isolated existence.
>
> *Condorcet*

Historical and Theoretical Foundations

The mounting intellectual and social changes in Central and
Western Europe discussed in previous chapters had, by the end of
the eighteenth century, begun to burst the seams of traditional educational institutions in many countries. Whether by revolution, as in
the American colonies and France, or by administrative decree of
autocratic rulers, as in Prussia and Russia, radically new programs
of formal education under public auspices were advanced and carried out. One of the seeming paradoxes in educational history is the
case of England, the leader in the industrial-social revolution and in
the application of empirical-utilitarian thought to education. But
England was one of the last major countries to sponsor a social
movement for a public system of education. This paradox is not
discussed here, but merely mentioned to invite further consideration
of England's exceptionality.[1]

The changes giving rise to conditions favoring public programs
of education can be traced, of course, at least as far back as the great
religious movements of the Reformation, and the expansion in trade
and manufacturing. Both Luther and Calvin obtained the support of
the civil authorities for their religious and educational reforms, and
the merchant class looked to magistrates and princes for aid in their
struggle against landed aristocracy to abolish trading restrictions
between regions and to expand markets abroad. The burghers either
joined the reformed schools movements that enjoyed state favor or,
in protest, set up their own schools to compete with the more tradi-

---

[1] Consult W. H. G. Armytage, *Four Hundred Years of English Education* (Cambridge: Cambridge University Press, 1963).

tional institutions. These protest groups in time came to demand outright state control over education so that their cultural interests might be fully recognized in society.

The scientific movement, too, with its naturalistic and materialistic interests, stood substantially outside ecclesiastical institutions, which continued to exercise educational leadership. Revolutionary findings in knowledge that did not seem to accommodate traditional religion had to look elsewhere for educational lodgings.

As the remnants of feudal aristocratic society made common cause with the churches, and as both played upon royalty for favor and influence, the forces of change had to construct new theories and means of action. A fourth major factor contributed its weight to these.

Nationalism as a social force, and as a growing element in the relations among sovereigns (who ruled by "divine right"), obliged kings and princes to consider their citizenry and national wealth as factors influencing the achievement of their policies. An individual's national loyalty as a Frenchman or Prussian became as important as that he pledged to his king. This ethnic and linguistic fact burst out upon Europe as a significant ideological component of change during the American and French revolutions. The human ingredients of this nationalism—the people—had certain claims, wants, and interests that they would insist their governments serve. Included among these was the demand for education under public control. The national power resulting from this new participation of the masses—and, in particular, the middle class—was evident in the tremendous outpouring of French strength throughout Europe for nearly a quarter of a century. Nationalism was indeed a new god, and it had to be acknowledged in the schools. The French example largely set the tone in continental Europe—and has since been extremely influential elsewhere. Although France herself did not realize until much later what her revolutionary tutors expected of her, the plans, ideas, and experiments that came with French tutorship and the period of French expansion have been of lasting influence.

The substantial changes which occurred in European societies as a result of revolutionary political, social, economic, and cultural movements gave rise to several fundamental educational problems that all "modernizing" countries have had to contend with in one way or another.

Nationalism and patriotism. *La patrie, der Vaterland, the Motherland, otechestvo*—all became in the nineteenth century symbols and appeals to citizen masses spread by popular proponents of a new sociopolitical order. Even monarchs and nobles had to rally to the new banner in order to broaden support for their rule. The individual henceforth identified with his nation, his country. Whether the identification was natural and appropriate or not, did not alter the ultimate purposes of those who saw clear advantages in the national solidarity and power that emerged from these nationalistic sentiments. Nationalism, and related patriotic themes tied to ethnic and linguistic kinship, could aid in solving many social and cultural problems lingering from feudalistic, ecclesiastical, and aristocratic social systems that the middle and laboring classes saw as obstacles to progress. The mass education of citizens under state control could be an agent of change in these endeavors. At least it could be used to weld together the many provincial sections of a nation-state by teaching a common language, literature, history, geography, and national purpose.

These features in the emerging citizens' schools in Europe reflected—and, indeed, were significantly shaped by—the currents of romanticism sweeping the continent in the early nineteenth century.[2] The French and American patriots who raised the banner of "republican ethics" were the first propagandists of the new cult. First in French schools, and later in American schools, the curricula included lessons in nationalism to inculcate a spirit of unity, brotherhood, and glory. In Prussia, leading thinkers sought to replace authoritarianism with nationalistic loyalty. This same trend can be seen in Russian writers, such as the Freemason Novikov, whose respect for the autocrat declined while that for the Russian nation took on new meaning.

Secularism and religion. The long and arduous struggle between church and state burst out in fiery conflict during the French Revolution, and thereafter periodically throughout the nineteenth century. Clerical privileges and temporalities were nearly destroyed at the height of republican France's power: church lands were sec-

---

[2] John S. Brubacher, *A History of the Problems of Education* (New York: McGraw-Hill Book Company, 1947), pp. 55–57.

ularized; the clergy came under state control and became subject to local election; and education was made pre-eminently a public responsibility. Similar developments had already occurred in many Protestant lands, but there a new union of the reformed churches and the public authorities resisted the secularization that spread over France and, to a lesser degree, republican America. In the United States religious orthodoxy and a religious oath were most often required of teachers.[3] Russia in the eighteenth century secularized much church land, gave leadership to the state in education, and made the clergy subject to government administration.

Paradoxically, the romantic national sentiments that followed republicanism, especially pronounced in France, helped traditional clerical forces to reassert themselves in national life and in education in particular. Although the national public system established during the republican and imperial regimes (in France) had left little place for clerical control of the schools, a resurgence of Jesuit and other church-inspired leadership culminated in the granting of great concessions to the Roman Catholic Church through legislation enacted in 1833, 1850, and 1851.[4] After France's defeat in 1870 by Prussia, a revival of republican forces led eventually to a reconstruction of public education, a full separation of church and state, and an end to clerical control in public education. One of the constant issues in the centuries-old battle between clerical and lay control of the schools was the conflict between modern standards and learning, on the one hand, and scholastic methods and classical learning on the other. Most states, however, have seen fit to preserve the private sector of education where churches and private agencies could offer educational programs free from public controls.

National Educational Organization and Theories

1. *The French Centralized System.* The Jesuit system, though dissolved in 1764, had been the only school organization approaching a national scope. La Salle's fine effort to introduce a system of primary schools (in the late seventeenth and early eighteenth cen-

---

[3] *Ibid.*, p. 334.
[4] Edward H. Reisner, *Nationalism and Education since 1789* (New York: The Macmillan Company, 1922), pp. 56–71.

turies) had been a bright light in French educational history, but shortlived. Some Calvinistic communities thrived for a time. Finance Minister Turgot (1727–81) advised King Louis XVI to establish a national council on education, but it took the revolutionary act of September 4, 1791, to authorize a "system of public instruction, common to all . . . and gratuitous with respect to . . . instruction . . . indispensable to all men."[5] This was a national appeal for citizens' education. The implementation of this provision was beset with great political obstacles created by the power struggles which followed the revolution. Although reforms in education were undertaken in 1793–95, drafters of legislation never saw either the full realization of their ideas or the funds that would have made such realization possible.

Perhaps the greatest synthesizer of republican, secular, and social egalitarian proposals for the new education was the Marquis de Condorcet (1743–94). Although of aristocratic birth, he was a republican and reformer in both theory and action. One of his major works, *Outline of an Historical Picture of the Progress of the Human Mind* (1795), tried to demonstrate with historical evidences that humanity is constantly moving toward perfection of the human condition, and that natural progress is a law of history. He delineated nine epochs of history, from primitive to contemporary social orders, and showed how obstacles to the improvement of the race are progressively overcome. It is the duty of historical study to find the roots of opposition to progress, particularly prejudices against change, and then to legislate new social institutions to erase these deficiencies. Inequalities of wealth, of wages, and of education are social legacies that must be eliminated in order to improve human culture. Constant improvement of institutions can thus be realized, according to this visionary. The next historical period of mankind, the tenth epoch, will see man's perfection—the paradise of the philosophers. For the future history of education, Condorcet offered a thesis: If education is made scientific and socially accessible to all, so that each individual rises to the highest level according to his merit, then mankind will constantly improve and perfect itself. The school would, in his opinion, play the key role in human culture. Condorcet, although leaning on many of the theoretical and his-

---

5 Gabriel Compayre, *The History of Pedagogy*, W. H. Payne, trans. (Boston: D. C. Heath & Company, 1901), p. 380.

torical works written by his predecessors, conceived a theory of sociocultural evolution—optimistic, to be sure—that anticipated in certain respects that of the social evolutionists of the nineteenth century.

To put his theory to work in the French Republic, Condorcet drew up educational legislation that would provide:

1. Universal primary education;
2. Middle (postprimary) schools;
3. Secondary (high) schools, or institutes;
4. Higher schools, called *lycées;*
5. A National Society of Sciences and the Arts (comparable to the present *Institut de France*).

The primary school would have the aim of providing the basic skills and culture necessary to the common citizen. For those unable to continue into secondary levels, adult education programs would be provided. Technical and vocational education would also be offered to advance knowledge of the practical arts and of the application of science to human affairs. Advancement up the school ladder toward higher education was based on merit and completely free of charge.

Condorcet's proposals were never voted upon, and similar legislative initiatives suffered from the political caprices of the new regime. Finally, on November 17, 1794, the Lakanal law—which provided a primary common school for each 1000 inhabitants—was passed. It required education in: the three basic skills, civil liberties and morals, French language, patriotism, and nature study. Boys and girls were educated separately; teachers were nominated by citizens and received state salaries. This legislation gave effect to the law of December, 1793, which made primary schooling compulsory for all children. Funds were sparingly provided for this program and later, under Napoleon, the lower schools were all but forgotten.[6]

During the period 1793–95, provisions were also made for teacher education, secondary schools, and institutions of higher learning. The establishment of normal schools, some of which have survived to this day, was one of the most forward-looking acts of the revolutionary period. But most of them did not last long. More fortunate were the secondary schools (at first called *central schools*) and the

---

[6] For the various proposals, including Condorcet's scheme, see the account based on original sources given in *ibid.*, pp. 380–407.

institutions of higher learning. In the secondary schools, modern and practical curricula took precedence over classical studies. Beginning in March, 1794, the government established a series of university-level institutes: the Central School of Public Works (i.e., the polytechnic school), for engineering; the higher Normal School; the School of Mars (for military affairs); the Conservatory of Arts; the Bureau of Longitudes; and the National Society. These great institutions, and their successors or derivatives, contributed much to the scientific and cultural advances made in France over the next hundred years. Most of them still exist.

Napoleon's government, little interested in citizens' primary education, devoted most of its energies to secondary and higher education. By imperial laws passed during the period 1806–11, the University of France (a national corporation, *not* a school) was established with jurisdiction over all public education and teaching. Completion of a state institution was required of applicants for teaching positions in the public system. Secondary colleges and lycées provided academic instruction in classics and mathematics in preparation for more advanced studies at the Faculties of Letters or Sciences, located in each academic district recognized by the national ministry of education. This development achieved national standardization of education—still the pattern in France—but access to secondary schools by lower and deprived social classes remained impossible until the enactment of primary school reforms.

The primary system did not receive attention until 1833, when Education Minister Guizot (1797–1874), stirred by the Prussian example, succeeded in getting legislation passed which provided for public primary schools with a practical curriculum. Gradually, the new system was put into effect.

Although the dreams of the revolutionaries and of the eighteenth century philosophers had faded, and although the restoration of the monarchial system and a return to conservative social forces pushed aside plans for social and cultural amelioration, French society had contributed much to human progress through education—not only in France, but also throughout Europe and in the New World. This fact can be readily seen in the ideas as well as in the educational developments in the American colonies before and after the American Revolution, although American culture developed a decentralized pattern, in contrast to the French passion for centralization.

2. *The German System.* Prussia's leading role in developing a national German system of education was asserted in the eighteenth and nineteenth centuries, although prior to that time strong traditions in German education (especially in the predominantly Lutheran states) had generally been established. The Reformation had brought the school into the arena of politics, where it came under both ecclesiastical and state controls. The Lutherans, seeking defense of their movement, insisted that magistrates and princes legislate educational as well as religious reform, and so the practice of public supervision was early begun.

School statutes (*Schuleordenung*) establishing the organization and content of education were issued by state authorities at various times in the sixteenth and seventeenth centuries, beginning with that of 1527–28 in Saxony.[7] German political thought, similar to English ideas, adopted the formula *jus circa sacra,* which recognized the right of the state to legislate concerning matters of establishing the faith, while in religious affairs per se the church was to be supreme. The jurisdictional path thus lay open in German lands for a public assertion of educational leadership.

By the early eighteenth century, Prussian kings and princes were exercising this leadership. In 1716–17, Frederick William ordered that all children attend school. A more solid legal basis was laid by Frederick II in 1763, when he issued the Prussian *General-Land-Schul-Reglement,* making common school attendance compulsory for children from five to thirteen or fourteen, when they would have mastered the primary instruction and religious lessons.[8] School maintenance was a parish responsibility, but the evidence indicates that the compulsory laws were imperfectly carried out. Concurrent with this movement was one, at first spasmodic, of creating teachers' seminaries; by the nineteenth century these had become a normal part of the Prussian scene.

The building of a general system of secondary and higher schools was not so deliberate or forthright a program as was that of the raising of the primary system. But a long tradition of secondary humanistic gymnasiums, derived from the early sixteenth century Reformation humanistic schools, as well as the older university tradition,

---

[7] Friedrich Paulsen, *German Education, Past and Present,* T. Lorenz, trans. (London: George Allen & Unwin, 1908), p. 58.

[8] *Ibid.,* p. 138.

endowed German education with one of the most complete three-level educational structures in Europe. Again, it was the Prussians who led; their 1794 Civil Code provided in no uncertain terms that education, from primary school to university, was a *state* responsibility. The energies expended in this effort during the eighteenth century gradually brought about the realization of this unequalled cultural concept. In practice and in law, Prussia and a few other German states carried out much of what the French *philosophes* and other thinkers, such as Rousseau, demanded of government in educational policies.

A few particular trends in German education had international significance: the humanistic—both idealistic and realistic—character of educational thought; the nature of university studies; and the cultural appeal to nationalism. Absorbing the pervading influences of French culture in the sixteenth and seventeenth centuries, many German intellectuals and educators experienced what might be called a local renaissance that gradually took on a national form. Lutheranism served to further this trend. That this process perhaps was not fully and rationally completed in Germany is not our concern here; rather, it is to point out a few leading ideas that highlighted the process and had special significance for education.

Both through the development of the German language and literature, and through a "religious" study of classical culture, German intellectuals in the eighteenth and early nineteenth centuries conceived of Greek classical culture as "the consummation and idealization of Nature and the Hellenic type of man as the full and unrestricted realization of the idea" of mankind.[9] It was the task of German educators, at least in part, to bring this ideal into being. German identification with these classical values emerged romantically through a flowering of German literature and philosophy, where in the great creativity of men such as Goethe and Kant, German idealism sensed its universal cultural aspirations. The school's task, then, was to prepare youth for the German cultural role in civilization. A prominent German interpreter of this movement, Heine, wrote that opposition to French materialism was the whole inspiration of German idealism, where "the spirit alone was recognized as a reality," and that "It almost seemed as though the spirit

---

[9] Paulsen, *op. cit.*, 161.

had sought on the German side of the Rhine revenge for the indignities that had been heaped upon it on the French side."[10] Literary humanism certainly had its place in this concept of the role of German culture.

Another main aspect of the German humanistic renaissance had a more naturalistic—and, in some respects, realistic—context. Influenced by the *philosophes* and naturalists, with their appeals for social and cultural reforms that would truly humanize and improve society, German thinkers such as Basedow (1723–90), Fichte (1762–1814), and Zeller (1774–1847), as well as a group of German and Swiss-German educators led by Pestalozzi (1746–1827), who had direct influences on most German thinkers of the time, advocated radically new solutions to the problem of national education. They saw the child *as* a child, and they insisted that pedagogy serve the individual needs and dispositions of childhood. Only through such a child-oriented (as opposed to an adult-oriented) method in education could teachers hope to develop and mold the new generation for the improvement of society. The interpretation of society's "best" interests varied, of course, with individual German thinkers. Fichte, for example, envisioned peculiarly nationalistic interests as supreme social goals in education. According to Fichte, although the school must "liberate" the moral, intellectual, physical, and vocational potential of the child, it must also engage in a higher aim—that of inculcating a national identity:

> It must here be obvious . . . that only the German—the original man . . . —really has a people and is entitled to count on one, and that he alone is capable of real and rational love for his nation. . . . It is the subjection in common to this special law that unites this mass in the eternal world, . . . to a natural totality permeated by itself.[11]

He preached that the individual had to find his true self in the larger whole—the nation—which was divinely fit to realize man's earthly and eternal destiny. Education must serve national morality,

---

[10] Heinrich Heine, *The Romantic School,* S. Fleishman, trans. (New York: Holt, Rinehart & Winston, Inc., 1882), pp. 118–19.

[11] Johan Gottlieb Fichte, *Addresses to the German Nation,* R. F. Jones and G. H. Turnbull, trans. (Chicago/London: The Open Court Publishing Co., 1922), pp. 130, 135. Used by permission of the Open Court Publishing Company. Fichte's appreciation for Pestalozzi and the values of his pedagogy for German needs was considerable.

and Pestalozzi's pedagogy was interpreted so as to contribute to this goal. The process of developing the child's nature would be conducted with national regeneration in mind—the making of Germans into leaders of European culture. In Fichte and similar thinkers, the new religion of nationalism tended to supplant Christianity and the traditional humanistic cult of the individual. But the author of *How Gertrude Teaches Her Children,* Pestalozzi, would reform society by bringing up youngsters in a new way, by teaching them in terms of their immediate intelligible world, of developing morally and intellectually free individuals, of socializing them through mutual love and respect.[12]

The growing and expanding Prussian primary school (*Volksschule*) was in need of practical pedagogical ideas, and these precepts as well as experiments based on them (carried on largely at Yverdon, in Switzerland) attracted many German educators and thinkers. Among them was Friedrich Fröbel (1782–1852), who later developed the kindergarten plan involving toys and games. But if Pestalozzi was vague and inadequate in providing a formal structure and theory for his ideas, German authorities put into practice many aspects of his school. Under Prussian leadership and its Ministers of Education (from 1808 on), they hoped to raise the cultural level of the masses and thus to enrich the state.[13] For several decades feverish efforts were launched to prepare teachers and schools for the new task. Such progress was made in general education and in teacher training that observers from France and the United States published extensive accounts to influence their own countries.

In the field of higher education, also, German progress was real and exemplary. After a relative decline in the quality of university studies following the Reformation, there occurred in a number of universities—especially at those (such as Halle) which were newly founded or reorganized—a new spirit of teaching and investigation. Departing somewhat from the lingering traditions of the scholastic method, professors introduced modern philosophic inquiry and scientific subjects, while making theological studies more practical, more social, and—in a sense—more subjective. For example, Christian Thomasius (at Halle, 1691–1727) emphasized human salvation

---

12 A summary of Pestalozzi's educational ideas is in Robert R. Rusk, *The Doctrines of the Great Educators* (London: Macmillan & Co., Ltd., 1954).

13 Paulsen, *op. cit.*, pp. 239–44.

and the living of one's religion, rather than high speculative concepts and human damnation. These tendencies increased under benevolent Prussian administration in the eighteenth century and most German universities, including those under Catholic control, felt the new influences. Lectures were delivered in German, and presentation of new subject matter resulting from experimentation and analysis was introduced. Unlike the universities in France and England, where responsibilities for scientific research were largely assumed by the academies, German universities engaged more and more in pure scientific pursuits. In the early nineteenth century, the new University of Berlin (1810) became an arch-representative of this trend. Enjoying a large measure of autonomy, university faculties in Germany pushed these interests, developing new scientific departments according to their experience and interests, and devising advanced study methods (such as the seminar). Although sometimes suffering from adverse political climates, the universities continued to take on the character of centers of advanced teaching and research. Later, in the nineteenth and in the twentieth centuries, these features influenced higher education in France, Great Britain, Russia, and the United States. Particularly did American colleges undertake to include advanced (graduate) teaching and research as part of their academic responsibilities.[14] The growth of university enrollments in Germany over two generations (1830–1903) was very impressive, in terms of nineteenth-century conditions: from 15,870 to 37,677.[15] The German example had international significance.

The importance which German intellectual leaders placed on academic excellence in the new sciences as well as in basic humanities is seen in the Prussian decision in 1834 to require the gymnasium "leaving examination" (the famous *Abitur* exam, actually dating from 1788) as the only recognized admissions requirement testing the academic preparation of gymnasium graduates. This decision, although it helped to standardize and bring order into the Prussian educational system, had socially rigid aspects which the conservative, humanistic circles in German education used to the disadvantage of a new and growing academic area: the modern sciences.

---

14 R. Freeman Butts, *The College Charts Its Course* (New York: McGraw-Hill Book Company, 1939).

15 Paulsen, *op. cit.,* p. 193.

The German *realschule,* or modern scientific high school, was not providing students with the "universal" academic background which was a prerequisite for training in one of the professions or in a major university discipline. For over 100 years, the *realschule* had established a new and useful tradition in education, but its purposes were handicapped in practice by conservative policies until reforms could be effected. During this time, the higher technical school (academy) developed in Germany for which the *realschule* served as a feeder. Technical school enrollments reached 10,000 by 1910.

The very practical contributions of the *realschule,* the research-oriented universities, and the technical schools can be seen in the very high place that German science and technology have occupied in the world over the past two generations. These real contributions, plus the welding together of the classical humanistic tradition and the nationalistic aim to inculcate new moral and cultural purposes in the education of German youth, mark the main characteristics of German education until recent times. By providing a solid elementary school base for the masses, by taking the lead in scientific learning and in research, and by expanding university education at a steady rate, Prussia—and then Germany as a whole—did much to fulfill the expectations of the eighteenth-century optimists and republican thinkers who dreamed of national systems of education as one of the main foundations of the modern state and its power. Germany's examples have influenced most of those countries that have sought industrial and technological progress and the reconstruction of their culture and society on new social and intellectual foundations.

3. National system in imperial Russia. Although Russia was one of the last great European states to experience the many influences of the Renaissance and the Reformation, she was one of the first to take action leading to national administration of schools. Looking at Russia's relatively late historical development within the community of Judeo-Christian, Greco-Roman traditions of culture, and considering her special role as a part of the Western tradition, one may well be surprised at the early emergence in Russia of a national system of education.

Eastern Slavdom (Russians, Ukrainians, Belorussians) received its higher literary and intellectual culture, as did other nations of Europe, from the classical and Christian world of Mediterranean civilization. Thus the Eastern Slavs are part of the European tradition, and all the more so when we recognize the common cultural debt that both Eastern and Western Europe owed to Byzantium as a source of classical and Christian learning. Of course, important differences between the two geographic areas must not be overlooked, any more than one would want to overlook differences within what is called the West European community (absolutist and parliamentary, Catholic and Protestant, and so on, because of their adherence to a common tradition).

Largely through highly centralized and autocratic rule, Russian government in the seventeenth and eighteenth centuries began to adopt certain cultural and educational practices accepted in Central and Western Europe. Under Tsar Aleksei Romanov (1645–76), educational and literary influences, such as the introduction of critical methods of teaching and research and the use of drama, came to be accepted.[16] These influences, and others coming from a growing colony of Western Europeans in Russia, made the social leaders of Moscow's domain increasingly aware of Western humanism, legal principles, scientific thought, and technical and economic progress. These were values which, in terms of organizing human existence and advancing a nation's power, showed the Russians to be in a comparatively unfavorable position. The overcoming of this situation became a central policy of the Russian crown, particularly from the time of Peter I (1689–1725).[17]

As a youth, Peter lived among the foreign merchants, adventurers, and religious representatives in Moscow; he learned their ways and came to know of the cultural advantages that would be derived from them. After an extended study trip to Western Europe, he undertook a series of reforms in economic, social, administrative, religious, and educational matters that set Russian society in a new cultural direction. Imperial laws in 1701, 1714, 1722, and 1724 laid the legal basis for a national network of educational institutions ranging from writing and arithmetic schools to a national Academy

---

16 Alexander Vucinich, *Science in Russian Culture* (Stanford, Calif.: Stanford University Press, 1963), pp. 16–37; and Chapters II and III, Medlin, *op. cit.,* pp. 153 ff.; *La Comédie d'Artaxèrxes,* in *Bibliothèque de l'Institut Français de Léningrad,* T. XXVIII (Paris: Institut d'Etudes Slaves, 1954).

17 The discussion that follows on imperial policies in education is based on Nicholas Hans, *History of Russian Educational Policy (1701–1917)* (London: P. S. King & Son, Ltd., 1931); and William H. E. Johnson, *Russia's Educational Heritage* (Pittsburgh: Carnegie Press, 1950).

of Sciences designed for advanced research. Most important for the growth of a national education system was the 1714 law requiring every imperial province to establish schools for mathematics, to which the nobility must send their sons. Although Peter's legislation was only partially carried out, and although later rulers did not always pursue his policies, a real beginning had been made in founding a national education system.

Under Catherine II (1762–96), new educational policies brought about the formation of a national Main Administration of Schools, directly responsible to the crown and in charge of all public educational institutions. Under the administrative plan, elementary and secondary schools were to be established in every province. By 1792, forty-one of the fifty provinces did, in fact, have a secondary-type school. Although access to these schools was open and free, the enserfed peasantry hardly had any such opportunity. But the Russian state, largely because of the influence of French reformist social thought, did acknowledge the principle of a unified and socially unrestricted national school system.

Further reforms under Alexander I (1801–25) provided for a national Ministry of Public Instruction (1804) and a system of six universities which served, as under the French imperial system, to supervise educational affairs within the university circuit. Legislation called for a socially democratic ladder system from lower secondary school to the university, but it did not provide for elementary education for the masses—the vast majority of whom were still enserfed or obliged to work on estates from generation to generation. Higher educational institutions were expanded in the 1820's and 1830's to include many technical and scientific fields, while the traditional academic universities remained intellectually and socially exclusive.

Beginning in the mid-nineteenth century, increasing social and political pressures in Russian society forced the tsars and their noble and clerical advisers to expand the base of the public education edifice. Local initiatives through the new *zemstva* (land councils) contributed a great deal to the broadening of primary education. Technical, scientific, and vocational education appeared at secondary levels, either as schools of the Ministry of Public Instruction or as special institutions under an economic ministry (communications, agriculture, and so on). The numbers actually enrolled in these new programs prior to the 1917 Revolution were, however, small in relation to the actual needs of the Russian Empire. Thus, although the Russian government did provide for a diversified and, in some respects, remarkable system of national education, the social traditions and old cultural values that largely governed society impeded any rapid progress through the system.

A number of outstanding Russian educational thinkers, who were —for the most part—radical, socialist leaders who opposed imperial policies, contributed a very significant literature on the need for a national education system. Belinskii, Herzen, Chernyshevskii, and Ushinskii (a political moderate) all agreed that education should be universal and free; that it should emphasize the modern Russian language (instead of medieval Russian or a foreign tongue, such as French); that it should stress practical knowledge and scientific teachings of the modern world; and that it should teach civic morality and nationalism. These were the main ingredients of a modern national education program. Only gradually did this content see the light of day in Russian education, and its full realization had to await the period of Soviet rule, when a radical emphasis on Communistic teachings was added to the recipe.

Seen in perspective over a two-hundred-year period, however, the development of a national system of education in Russia, resembling closely other European systems of a centralized character, stood as an accomplished fact by the twentieth century. Its use in recent decades by a vigorous leadership to implement a scientific and technical revolution in Russian culture has brought it to the forefront among modern national systems. Not only has the Soviet system been successful for educational changes in European Russia, but it also has made significant progress among the culturally backward peoples inherited from the Russian colonial empire. These achievements of the Russian educational system attract attention and invite us to study more carefully than we have in the past the historical resources of that national system.

4. The American decentralized system. By virtue of its early colonization, North America was a territory of many cultures and many ethnic groups. Even within the eventually dominant Anglo-Saxon, English-speaking regions, religious, political, and social differences made homogeneity in educational practices impossible. A heritage of diversity and decentralization thus stamped the colonies, and later the United States. Local community control (joint state-church control) in the North, private and denominational control in the middle colonies, and mixed denominational and home control in the South explain the pattern.[18]

The most dynamic educational concept obtained in the North, where in Calvinist tradition the community and its church jointly operated town and village schools for religious and practical purposes. It was the local council, however, that was the constituting authority, and this practice established the tradition of public control over compulsory schooling early in American history (1642–47 in Massachusetts). Before the secularizing American Revolution, therefore, the public school was part of the culture. With the spread of new knowledge and egalitarian, representative social theories, movements arose to make the schools instruments of progress.

Although the community-controlled public school system as developed in the north offered (especially as its influence spread) a model for dissemination of modern knowledge, by and large those social groups who managed to run the schools were not disposed to the new knowledge. Modernizing intellectual movements were too urbane, too sophisticated. The cultural innovations they sought were resisted. In the main their adherents represented one of three schools of thought.[19] The Naturalists, or Deists, saw the world as quite free from traditional religious bonds and supernatural influences (not to say superstitions). That God or the Supreme Being had set the universe in motion—yes, that was logical. But He laid down his laws once and for all, leaving mankind to master them and to build a civilization in accord with scientific, natural laws. Religious dogma, then, had no place in human culture nor in education. Benjamin Franklin, Thomas Jefferson, Ethan Allen, and Samuel Johnson were latter eighteenth century followers of this line of thought. Strong French intellectual influences lay behind their thinking.

The "materialists," fewer in number and of lesser influence, did not try to accommodate deistic principles in their world view, although they usually acknowledged a divine force as an original

---

[18] See F. Butts and L. Cremin, *A History of Education in American Culture* (New York: Holt, Rinehart & Winston, Inc., 1959), Chaps. 3–4.

[19] For background on American intellectual rebels, consult H. W. Schneider, *A History of American Philosophy* (New York: Columbia University Press, 1947), Chap. 2; Max Savelle, *The Seeds of Liberty* (New York: Alfred A. Knopf, Inc., 1948).

cause. Reality in this view is entirely material, dependent on matter and its development. Scientific and experimental methods are the only true source of knowledge.

These were the main radical schools in eighteenth and early nineteenth century American thought, although the "Common Sense" thinkers, such as J. Witherspoon, attempted to compromise between traditional religious cosmology and the new science. The puritan, self-reliant character took to this middle-of-the-road attitude in a pragmatic way, keeping a foot in both camps, and in time this "uncommitted" philosophy seems best to have represented native American thought.

All these thinkers looked kindly at reform in education aimed at departing from a narrow humanistic-religious-philosophical program toward a program including modern languages, science, and practical studies. Franklin's attempt at founding a new Academy at Philadelphia (1749–51) demonstrated the new educational thought at mid-century: that education should "bake bread"—i.e., be useful and practical. But tradition was still too strong and, as Franklin lamented, "the Latinists were combined" against him. Jefferson, in his plan for universal primary education and for selected schooling for bright boys at secondary and college levels, anticipated some of the legislation in revolutionary France. He also would have a modern curriculum, with practical mathematics, sciences, history, and modern languages in the program.

Although these and similar efforts had some influence in new, private academies founded to meet growing commercial needs, American education changed little until well after the Revolution and the turn of the century. The secularizing influences of the federal and state constitutions, together with those fostered by the radical intellectual movements and by urban economic interests, brought about new demands on the schools. The quickest to respond were the private academies, which sent their graduates not only to colleges but also into specialized jobs and trades.

The colleges, nine in number by the time the colonies achieved nationhood, retained essentially their purposes of training ministers and lawyers, although as early as 1787 Harvard College employed a professor of French. By the first decade of the nineteenth century, every state had one or more colleges, and there can be recognized in that development a kind of higher education "system." The colleges did not compare with European universities in scholarship, but Harvard's library (some twelve thousand volumes about 1790) showed a good beginning.[20] Their internal organization, except for the Jesuit school at Georgetown, had not departed essentially from academic plans of English universities. Total graduations up to 1800, for all the states, amounted to a total of 9144.

Unlike the French Revolution, which thrust public education to the forefront of cultural action, the American social movement did not espouse the public school. In fact, no direct reference to education was made in the federal Constitution, although Congress passed land ordinances (1785, 1787) which provided financial assistance to education in new territories. In 1819, the Federal Government, through the famous Darmouth Case, asserted the right of private and religious bodies to maintain educational institutions.

With this diverse pattern, with the absence of national cultural leadership, and with the relatively unstable conditions that existed in the new state, there was little initiative to provide a coherent system of public education. But in the period termed *The Awakening,* especially the decades after the War of 1812, conditions and sources of leadership produced new possibilities, especially in the Northern and Central regions. Commercial and industrial growth, and colonization in the West, created new social problems as well as classes that needed attention in some way. Popular rights, claimed against local religious and propertied restrictions, received political consideration; one of these rights included a tax-supported school.

In the 1820's and 1830's, New England and New York led the way with reforms in primary, secondary, and teacher education.[21] The names of Clinton, Carter, Mann, and Barnard are among those who labored long to reassert public responsibility for popular education and teachers. Much of the pedagogical theory and concepts of school organization derived from Prussian and French experience. Through Horace Mann (1796–1859), as the prime example, modernizing European trends, especially Prussian, were infused into

---

[20] Louis Shores, *Origins of the American College Library, 1638–1800* (Nashville: George Peabody College, 1934), p. 56. On higher education for the time, consult Walter Crosby Eells, *Baccalaureate Degrees,* Circular No. 528 (Washington, D.C.: U.S. Department of Health, Education, and Welfare, Office of Education, May 1958), p. 22.

[21] This section on American educational developments is largely based on Butts and Cremin, *op. cit.;* and E. P. Cubberley, *Public Education in the United States* (Boston: Houghton Mifflin Company, 1934).

the American educational stream. Although the evidence suggests that these influences did not affect the schools until some decades later, the campaign waged by Mann and his followers did much to bring local authorities to organize statewide systems of public education. Mann made history as the first chief state school officer (Secretary of the Board of Education of Massachusetts) in 1837. The office of city superintendent had developed earlier, but thereafter both types of administrators began to perform statistical and advisory services important to the development of school programs.

Legislative and financial support for public primary education became a fact in most states by 1860, and in all after the Civil War. Compulsory school attendance and special educational services for the unfortunate were passed into law by states from the latter 1860's into the 1870's and 1880's. As primary grades grew in number, the tendency was to provide postprimary education at public expense and under state control. Although the public high school dates from the English High School in Boston (1821), it did not displace the private academies in importance and numbers until after 1870, when public tax monies became valid sources for public secondary education. As public authorities gained control over secondary schools, the latter began to offer more and more practical studies useful to the average citizen. By the end of the century, the American high school was no longer only an academic preparation for the university, as in Europe. It had gone a good distance to becoming the comprehensive institution that provided education to all youth who sought practical skills and useful knowledge. On a national scale, the public high school had grown into the "system."

Concurrent with the expansion of primary and secondary public schools was the teacher education movement: the city, county, and state normal school, also a product of New England experience (with European inspiration), became a nationally accepted agency for teacher education after mid-century. Many reformers saw women filling naturally the new role of public school teacher, and normal schools reflected this view.

In higher education, a steady if unimpressive change worked itself into curriculum and organization. Both European (again, especially German) and native ideas were drawn upon. At home, the idea of a farmers-mechanics high school or college fired the imagination of some leaders—for example, Congressman Morrill, who in 1862 brought about passage of a federal act that would finance "land grant" colleges for practical, scientific studies in every state of the union. Most of these higher schools have since become the great state universities that now lead in experimental and professional education. The new German influence showed itself in the acceptance of the idea of advanced studies and research as a normal part of university education. A place for science and investigation can be traced, of course, back to the Enlightenment, but its educational manifestation was a product of German universities. At Harvard, Columbia, Johns Hopkins, and Michigan, for example, university presidents waged a hard battle for modern teachings, professional preparation of specialists, and advanced research work as parts of a university's academic business.[22]

These efforts were largely successful and they placed the American educational system in a most productive and mobile position—an enviable one among modern nations. One of the key links in the growing success of American higher education has been the autonomy which governing boards (regents) have granted private and some public institutions. Most often these boards, nonacademic in composition, have well represented the interests of society and served as sources of financial support, so that the American college and university have been closely related to the concerns of society. At the same time, the feeling has grown in some quarters that these relationships have, in time, worked against the intellectual pursuits properly assigned to university life.

As a kind of capstone—more decorative than functional—to the American system has been the U.S. Office of Education, in Washington, D.C. Established in 1867 to perform statistical reporting services and to help administer a few federally financed institutions, the Office differed markedly from European ministries of education which controlled and administered educational programs. In the United States, the local state and district authorities have always exercised these powers. Nonetheless, the Office has performed invaluable services in collecting statistics, making surveys, and providing consultant services that are not easily accessible to the local authorities. Most annual reports of the Commissioner of Education

---

[22] Butts, *op. cit.*, pp. 129–250.

to Congress have, for nearly one hundred years, contained reports or information on education in other countries.

In some respects, the decentralized American system, from elementary school to the state university, fulfilled hopes of the eighteenth century dreamers who called for a national educational program accessible to talented and willing youth of all classes.

Bibliography

Barclay, William, *Educational Ideals in the Ancient World*. London: Collins, 1959.

Baynes, Norman and H. Moss, *Byzantium*, rev. ed. Oxford: Oxford University Press, 1949.

Brinton, Crane, *The Shaping of the Modern Mind*. New York: The New American Library, 1957.

Brubacher, John S., *A History of the Problems of Education*. New York: McGraw-Hill Book Company, 1947.

Butts, R. Freeman, *A Cultural History of Education*. New York: The Macmillan Company, 1955.

Compayre, Gabriel, *The History of Pedagogy*. W. H. Payne, trans. Boston: D. C. Heath & Company, 1901.

Fowler, W. S., *The Development of Scientific Method*. Oxford: Pergamon Press, 1962.

Hall, A. R., *The Scientific Revolution: 1500–1800*. London: Longmans, Green & Company, Ltd., 1954.

Kandel, Isaac L., *History of Secondary Education*. Boston: Houghton Mifflin Company, 1930.

Kane, W. T., *History of Education*. Chicago: Loyola University Press, 1938.

Konstantinov, N. A., *Istoriia pedagogiki*. Moscow: Akademiia Ped. Nauk, 1959.

Laistner, M. L. W., *Thought and Letters in Western Europe*, A.D. *500 to* A.D. *900*, 2nd ed. Ithaca, N. Y.: Cornell University Press, 1957.

Marrou, Henri I., *A History of Education in Antiquity*, G. Lamb, trans. New York: Sheed & Ward, 1956.

Mulhern, James, *A History of Education*. New York: The Ronald Press Company, 1959.

Reisner, Edward H., *Nationalism and Education since 1789*. New York: The Macmillan Company, 1922.

Riché, Pierre, *Education et culture dans l'occident barbare, VIe–VIIIe siècles, Patristica Sorbonensia, No. 4*. Paris: Editions du Seuil, 1962.

Rusk, Robert R., *The Doctrines of the Great Educators*. London: Macmillan & Co., Ltd., 1954.

Shalaby, Ahmad, *History of Muslim Education*. Beirut: Dar Alkashaf, 1954.

Van Dalen, D. B., *A World History of Physical Education*. Englewood Cliffs, N.J.: Prentice-Hall, Inc., 1958.

Note: for wider, more detailed, and more original sources, the reader is referred to the footnotes in this survey, and to the standard guides to literature in educational, cultural, and social history covering special periods, areas, and problems; and also to guides to special topics and disciplines in the general field of education.

Index